Double Squeezes

This is the third volume in the mini-series on squeeze play planned by grand master Hugh Kelsey. It deals with one of the most exciting and fulfilling plays in the game—the double squeeze, in which both opponents come under pressure, either at the same time or on consecutive tricks. If you find it fun to put one defender through the mincer, you will enjoy even more making both of them suffer. There is nothing, the author says in his introduction, to match the thrill of planning a double squeeze and bringing it to a successful conclusion.

And yet the techniques involved are so simple that they can be mastered by any competent player. It is largely a matter of recognising the possibilities in good time and knowing the right moves to make. The right moves are set out in this book by Kelsey with his customary clarity of expression, and a host of fascinating hands and diagrams lay bare the secrets of the double squeeze in all its guises.

The improving player, the aspiring player and the expert will all find something in this book to add distinction and lustre to their game, resulting in more wins, increased confidence and great satisfaction.

Double Squeezes

HUGH KELSEY

LONDON
VICTOR GOLLANCZ LTD
in association with Peter Crawley
1987

First published in Great Britain 1987
by Victor Gollancz Ltd,
14 Henrietta Street, London WC2E 8QJ

© Hugh Kelsey 1987

British Library Cataloguing in Publication Data
Kelsey, H.W.
  Double squeezes.—(Master bridge series).
  —(Kelsey on squeeze play).
  1. Contract bridge—Squeeze
  I. Title II. Series III. Series
  795.41·53   GV1282.44

ISBN 0–575–04115–3

Photoset and printed in Great Britain by
WBC Print Ltd, Bristol

Contents

Introduction

The earlier books in this series, *Simple Squeezes* and *Strip-Squeezes*, dealt with the squeezing of one opponent in two suits. The basic forms provide the right introduction to the subject since the simple squeezes are the ones most often encountered in practical play.

Now it is time to widen our horizons. There are many hands on which success can be achieved only by squeezing *both* defenders. This may sound a formidable undertaking but I hope to show that it is not really so. A double squeeze is just a combination of two simple squeezes—one against each opponent—and the play of the hand is usually far from difficult. Players who have acquired a knowledge of basic squeeze technique soon learn to recognise the special arrangements of entries and menaces that are needed to make a double squeeze effective.

In one way the problem is simplified for, with rare exceptions, the double squeeze operates only at the primary or direct level. To squeeze both opponents declarer must be in a position to win all the remaining tricks but one at the time when the squeeze card is led. If there is more than one loser, declarer must rectify the count by conceding the required number of tricks to the opponents at an earlier stage.

Nothing that is worth doing comes easily. An improvement in squeeze technique can be won only at the cost of some effort since there are new positions to learn, each with its own configuration of entries and menaces. Players with the ability to think their way through each problem from first principles are thin on the ground. The only way to be sure of recognising double squeeze positions when they arise is to study example hands in advance.

Is the labour worth while? Those familiar with the increased profit and pleasure that squeeze play can bring will entertain no doubts on the matter. Having tasted the delights of putting one opponent through the mincer, they will surely wish to extend the experience to include both opponents. There is no greater thrill in the game than deliberately planning a double squeeze and bringing the play to a successful conclusion.

Acquiring a knowledge of double squeeze technique will bring increased confidence in your card-playing ability. It will make you a more respected partner and a more feared opponent.

1

The Positional Double Squeeze

In simple squeeze play two menaces are required, one of which must be a two-card menace consisting of a winner and a loser. For the double squeeze, which is a combination of two simple squeezes, an extra menace is needed. The minimum requirements are two one-card menaces (one threatening each opponent) and a two-card menace against both opponents. In the most common form both opponents are squeezed at the same trick. We can call this a 'simultaneous' double squeeze. Here is a basic diagram:

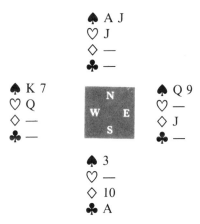

When the ace of clubs is played, West has to discard a spade in order to keep the queen of hearts. The heart jack, having done its job, is discarded from the table, and East is immediately squeezed in spades and diamonds.

In the diagram it can easily be seen that this double squeeze is made up of a simple positional squeeze against West and a simple automatic squeeze against East. Is it more difficult to execute than a simple squeeze? Only marginally. Declarer has to watch out for the master cards in both hearts and diamonds.

This is the correct procedure in all double squeeze play. Watch out for the cards that can beat your one-card menaces and leave the double menace to look after itself.

Obviously there is not room for all three menaces to lie in the same hand. The diagram arrangement is common, where a one-card menace is with the squeeze card and the other two menaces are in the opposite hand. But note that the one-card menaces must lie 'over' the opponents they threaten. Interchange the queen of hearts and the jack of diamonds in the last diagram and the squeeze does not work, since dummy has to discard ahead of East.

EXTENSIONS

The one-card menace against the opponent to the right of the squeeze card may be increased in length by the addition of a winner without detracting from the force of the squeeze.

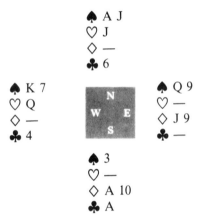

The only difference is that the squeeze becomes sequential instead of simultaneous. When the ace of clubs is played West feels no pressure, but East is obliged to part with a spade in order to keep his diamond guard. At the next trick the play of the diamond ace squeezes West in the majors.

Although this sequence of play is permissible, those with a real feeling for squeeze play will prefer to avoid all ambiguity by cashing the ace of diamonds first. The ace of clubs then squeezes both opponents simultaneously.

An extension to the one-card menace against the opponent to the left of the squeeze card is not allowable in positional squeeze play. The reason can be clearly seen in the next diagram.

[10]

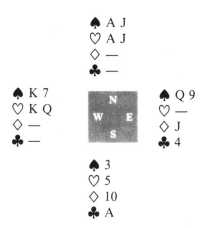

♠ A J
♡ A J
◊ —
♣ —

♠ K 7   ♠ Q 9
♡ K Q   ♡ —
◊ —   ◊ J
♣ —   ♣ 4

♠ 3
♡ 5
◊ 10
♣ A

On the play of the ace of clubs West has to throw a spade in order to keep his hearts. The jack of hearts can be thrown from dummy, but there is no subsequent squeeze against East. When a heart is played to the ace East can afford to throw the diamond jack, since declarer no longer has any communication with his own hand.

To bring off a double squeeze declarer would need to have cashed the ace of hearts at an earlier stage in the play.

TIMING

Double squeeze timing has to be exact. In a 3-card ending declarer must be in a position to win two tricks, and in a 4-card ending he must be able to win three tricks. If there is more than one loser when the squeeze card is led, the squeeze will not get off the ground. Extend the diagram on page 9 by giving each player a small diamond, for instance, and there is no chance of a successful squeeze.

When declarer cashes the ace of clubs in the new diagram, neither defender comes under any pressure. Everyone discards

♠ A J
♡ J
◊ 3
♣ —

♠ K 7   ♠ Q 9
♡ Q   ♡ —
◊ 4   ◊ J 7
♣ —   ♣ —

♠ 3
♡ —
◊ 10 6
♣ A

diamonds, and declarer can find no winning line of play.

Clearly the loser count is a vital factor in the execution of a double squeeze. The correct timing sometimes arrives automatically, for in the natural course of trying to defeat the contract the defenders often cash the tricks that are rightfully theirs, leaving declarer to struggle for the remainder. Here is an example.

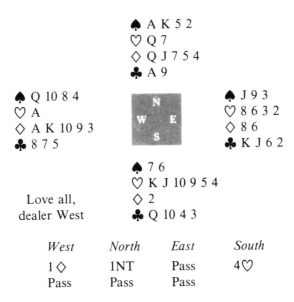

```
              ♠ A K 5 2
              ♡ Q 7
              ◇ Q J 7 5 4
              ♣ A 9
♠ Q 10 8 4                      ♠ J 9 3
♡ A                            ♡ 8 6 3 2
◇ A K 10 9 3                    ◇ 8 6
♣ 8 7 5                        ♣ K J 6 2
              ♠ 7 6
              ♡ K J 10 9 5 4
Love all,     ◇ 2
dealer West   ♣ Q 10 4 3
```

West	North	East	South
1◇	1NT	Pass	4♡
Pass	Pass	Pass	

The opening lead is the ace of diamonds on which East plays the eight. West cashes the ace of hearts and then switches to the four of spades. Winning with dummy's ace, you play the ace of clubs followed by the nine. East goes up with the king and returns a trump, on which West discards a club.

So East was not willing to let you ruff a club on the table. That's no big surprise. Now, unless the club jack drops, you appear to be a trick short. But there is no need to despair, for the game is virtually assured on a double squeeze. East is marked with the clubs, so the club ten will act as a one-card menace against him. In the queen of diamonds you have a one-card menace against West, and the spades will serve as the double menace.

What preparations are needed? None at all. The defenders have scored their three tricks and you are in a position to take all the rest except one. The timing is right and the defenders will be unable to escape the pressure. Draw trumps, cash the club queen, and continue trumps to reach the diagram position:

On the play of the last heart West has to discard a spade in order to keep his diamond. The diamond is thrown from the table and East, in his turn, is squeezed in the black suits.

There was nothing very diffi-

♠ K 5
♡ —
♢ Q
♣ —

♠ Q 10   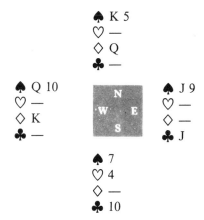   ♠ J 9
♡ —   ♡ —
♢ K   ♢ —
♣ —   ♣ J

♠ 7
♡ 4
♢ —
♣ 10

cult about the play of this hand, but a declarer unaware of the double squeeze potential might have done something to ruin the ending.

EXTENDING THE DOUBLE MENACE

♠ A K 5
♡ —
♢ Q
♣ —

♠ Q 10 8   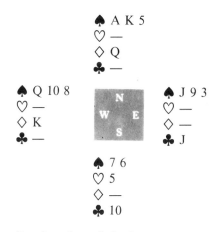   ♠ J 9 3
♡ —   ♡ —
♢ K   ♢ —
♣ —   ♣ J

♠ 7 6
♡ 5
♢ —
♣ 10

An extra winner may accompany the long menace without spoiling the squeeze. Suppose, in the last hand, that after cashing the ace of hearts West switches to a club. The king wins and a trump comes back.

There is no real difference in the routine. You draw trumps, unblock the club ace, ruff a diamond and play your last trump. This time it is a 4-card ending.

On the play of the last trump both defenders are squeezed as before.

RECTIFYING THE COUNT

The correct timing may arrive on a plate in certain cases, but at other times you will have to make a conscious effort to adjust the loser-count.

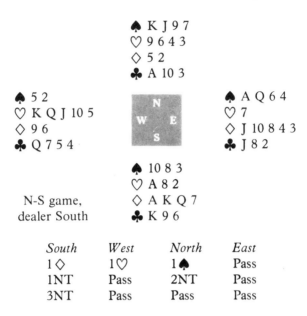

♠ K J 9 7
♡ 9 6 4 3
◇ 5 2
♣ A 10 3

♠ 5 2
♡ K Q J 10 5
◇ 9 6
♣ Q 7 5 4

♠ A Q 6 4
♡ 7
◇ J 10 8 4 3
♣ J 8 2

♠ 10 8 3
♡ A 8 2
◇ A K Q 7
♣ K 9 6

N-S game,
dealer South

South	West	North	East
1◇	1♡	1♠	Pass
1NT	Pass	2NT	Pass
3NT	Pass	Pass	Pass

West leads the king of hearts and you allow him to hold the trick. Next comes the queen of hearts on which East discards a spade. How should you plan the play?

You have to hope that East has the ace of spades, and there may seem little point in holding up again in hearts. If West has the spade queen you will make nine tricks easily enough. But there is always the possibility that East will have both spade honours. In that case you will be a trick short and will have to rely on a squeeze. As a matter of normal technique you should hold up again in hearts in order to rectify the count.

West continues with a third heart to your ace and East discards a diamond. You run the eight of spades, losing to the queen, win the diamond return and play another spade, which wins the trick. East takes his spade ace on the third round and returns a second diamond.

Now the double squeeze is marked on the assumption that East has the long diamonds. You have a heart menace against West and a diamond menace against East, so when it comes to the crunch neither defender will be able to guard the clubs. Winners accompanying the one-card menaces should be played off before setting a double squeeze in motion, so you cash your top diamond, discarding a club from dummy. Then cross to the ace of clubs and play the last spade in the diagram position.

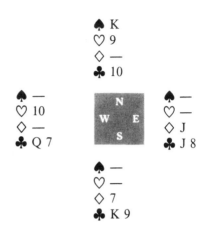

♠ K
♡ 9
♢ —
♣ 10

♠ —
♡ 10
♢ —
♣ Q 7

♠ —
♡ —
♢ J
♣ J 8

♠ —
♡ —
♢ 7
♣ K 9

This time the squeeze card is on the table and the long menace in your hand, but it makes no difference.

When the king of spades is played East has to part with a club in order to keep his diamond winner. You discard the seven of diamonds from hand, and West is unable to cope with the pressure in hearts and clubs.

ISOLATING A GUARD

The preparatory moves associated with simple squeeze technique can be equally useful in setting up a double squeeze. It may be necessary, for instance, to do some ruffing in order to isolate a single menace against one of the defenders.

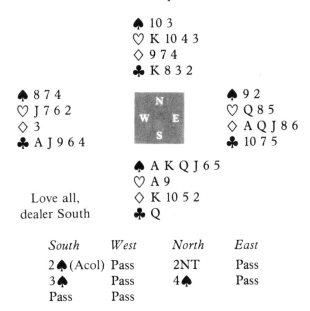

♠ 10 3
♡ K 10 4 3
◇ 9 7 4
♣ K 8 3 2

♠ 8 7 4
♡ J 7 6 2
◇ 3
♣ A J 9 6 4

♠ 9 2
♡ Q 8 5
◇ A Q J 8 6
♣ 10 7 5

♠ A K Q J 6 5
♡ A 9
◇ K 10 5 2
♣ Q

Love all,
dealer South

South	West	North	East
2♠ (Acol)	Pass	2NT	Pass
3♠	Pass	4♠	Pass
Pass	Pass		

West leads the three of diamonds, and when dummy goes down you see that three no-trumps would have been a simple contract. Still, four spades looks safe enough.

The picture changes when East wins the first trick with the ace of diamonds and returns the queen. The diamond king is ruffed away and West returns a trump. This leaves you with the problem of avoiding a further diamond loser.

What are the prospects? You need to find the ace of clubs with West and you must hope that he has length in the suit. You have a diamond menace against East, and if you can establish a club menace against West, neither defender will be able to keep hearts in the double-squeeze ending.

So you win the trump switch in hand and play the queen of clubs. West has to win, otherwise you can simply draw trumps and concede a diamond. The trump return is won in dummy and the king of clubs is played for a diamond discard (all side winners should be cashed early in positional double-squeeze play). The next move is to ruff a club in hand.

This removes East's last card in the suit and sets the scene for the double squeeze. The run of the trumps reduces the hand to the position shown in the diagram.

The last trump extracts a heart from West, and when the eight of clubs is discarded from the table East is squeezed in the red suits.

Note that the squeeze would have failed if you had not

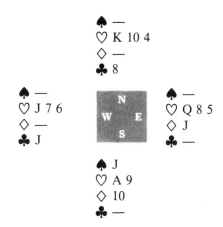

ruffed the third round of clubs. East would have kept the jack of diamonds and the ten of clubs, leaving his partner to take care of the third round of hearts.

A SPLIT 3-CARD MENACE

A second type of double squeeze is possible when the long menace is a split 3-card menace consisting of two winners and a loser. This

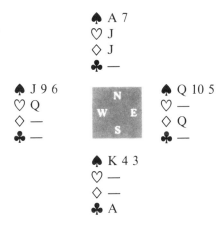

arrangement permits both one-card menaces to lie opposite the squeeze card.

The long menace lies in the same hand as the squeeze card with the single menaces in the opposite hand. Neither defender can hold the position when the ace of clubs is led.

This form of double squeeze is quite flexible in that it will work even if the East and West hands are interchanged. But it is still a positional squeeze. One of the menaces has to be discarded on the ace of clubs, and declarer has to know what he is doing. Otherwise he might discard the wrong jack on the squeeze card.

In practical play there is seldom any difficulty in determining which defender holds which suit.

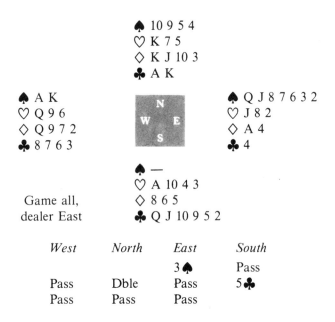

```
                    ♠ 10 9 5 4
                    ♡ K 7 5
                    ◇ K J 10 3
                    ♣ A K
   ♠ A K                                  ♠ Q J 8 7 6 3 2
   ♡ Q 9 6              N                  ♡ J 8 2
   ◇ Q 9 7 2        W       E             ◇ A 4
   ♣ 8 7 6 3            S                 ♣ 4
                    ♠ —
                    ♡ A 10 4 3
   Game all,        ◇ 8 6 5
   dealer East      ♣ Q J 10 9 5 2
```

West	North	East	South
		3 ♠	Pass
Pass	Dble	Pass	5 ♣
Pass	Pass	Pass	

After a pre-emptive opening from East and a sporting double from North, you arrive in the hazardous contract of five clubs.

West starts with the ace of spades. You ruff and play a diamond to dummy's ten. East takes his ace and returns a spade. How do you plan the play?

East is marked with long spades and West with the queen of diamonds. If the diamonds fail to break, there must be a good chance of a double squeeze with hearts as the long menace. However, both one-card menaces will be in dummy, which means that you cannot afford to break up your split menace in hearts. If you ruff the second spade you will be in trouble in the event of a 4–1 club break, which is not unlikely.

To give yourself a chance you must discard a heart on the second spade. This serves the dual purpose of retaining trump control and rectifying the count for your squeeze. West wins and is unable to continue the spade attack. Suppose he returns a diamond. You win with the jack and cash dummy's top clubs. When East shows out you can safely cash the king of diamonds, after which you return to hand with a spade ruff. West may try to escape his fate by under-ruffing but it makes no difference. You play out the trumps and reach this position:

The play of the ten of clubs forces West to disgorge a heart. The three of diamonds is thrown from the table and East faces a similar dilemma. Compelled to keep the queen of spades he also has to part with a heart, and your ten of hearts is good for the last trick.

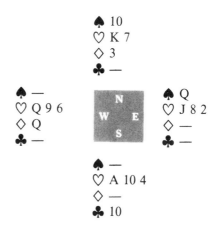

```
                    ♠ 10
                    ♡ K 7
                    ◇ 3
                    ♣ —
   ♠ —                          ♠ Q
   ♡ Q 9 6           N          ♡ J 8 2
   ◇ Q          W        E      ◇ —
   ♣ —              S          ♣ —
                    ♠ —
                    ♡ A 10 4
                    ◇ —
                    ♣ 10
```

REJECTING A FINESSE

A knowledge of double-squeeze technique will sometimes enable you to avoid a losing finesse. Consider this hand.

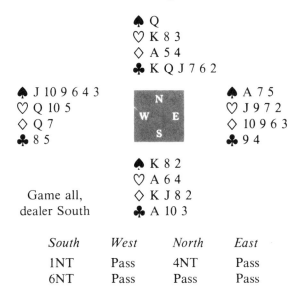

♠ Q
♥ K 8 3
♦ A 5 4
♣ K Q J 7 6 2

♠ J 10 9 6 4 3
♥ Q 10 5
♦ Q 7
♣ 8 5

♠ A 7 5
♥ J 9 7 2
♦ 10 9 6 3
♣ 9 4

♠ K 8 2
♥ A 6 4
♦ K J 8 2
♣ A 10 3

Game all,
dealer South

South	West	North	East
1NT	Pass	4NT	Pass
6NT	Pass	Pass	Pass

You open one no-trump and partner invites with a raise to four. Liking your controls, you bid the slam.

West leads the jack of spades to the queen and ace. East returns the seven of spades to your king. Wishing to keep the heart position flexible, you discard a small diamond from the table. What now?

You can count eleven top tricks, and at first glance it may seem reasonable enough to try the diamond finesse for the twelfth. But no squeeze player will dream of taking the diamond finesse. The eight of spades looks like a single menace against West, and if East has the queen of diamonds there is no need to finesse. A double squeeze, with hearts as the long menace, will bring home the slam without risk.

The right move is to cash the ace and king of diamonds before running the clubs. As it happens, the fall of the diamond queen solves all your problems. But if East had held the diamond queen you would still have been in good shape. The play of the clubs would have resulted in the ending shown in the diagram.

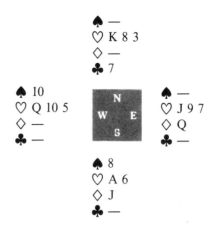

When the last club is played from dummy, East has to part with a heart. You throw the jack of diamonds from hand, and West has to succumb to the pressure in the majors.

CHOICE BETWEEN SIMPLE AND DOUBLE SQUEEZE

Perhaps too little was made of the decision you had to take on the last hand. It was not just a matter of choosing between finesse and squeeze. You also had to decide which *sort* of squeeze to aim for.

If you had reason to believe that West might have the queen of diamonds guarded, the only chance would have been a simple spade-diamond squeeze against West. This would require West to hold four diamonds, not very likely when he is marked with long spades. You would need to discard a heart from dummy at trick two, and then run the clubs followed by the top hearts. The end position is shown in the diagram.

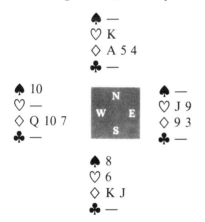

The play of the heart king squeezes West automatically in spades and diamonds.

Such decisions can be tricky, but there will usually be some evidence that points towards the winning line.

INVERSION

So far we have looked only at simultaneous double squeezes, where both defenders are squeezed on the same trick. In a sequential double squeeze the defender on the left of the squeeze card is flattened first and his partner on the next trick. In a positional squeeze it is not possible to squeeze the defender on the right of the squeeze card first.

A sequential double squeeze normally requires an inverted position where the squeeze card is in the same hand as the double menace. Both single menaces lie in the opposite hand, which holds no entry in the suit of the double menace. Naturally there must be a compensating entry elsewhere, and that entry takes the form of an extension to the one-card menace against the opponent to the left of the squeeze card.

Here is the basic diagram.

There is a two-card double menace in hearts, a two-card menace in spades against West and a one-card menace in diamonds against East. The ace of spades provides the necessary communication between the hands.

When the ace of clubs is played, West has to discard a heart in order to keep his spade guard. The seven of spades is thrown from dummy and East discards his spade without pain. But on

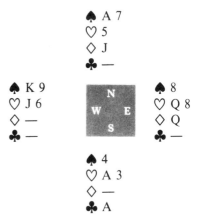

          ♠ A 7
          ♡ 5
          ◇ J
          ♣ —

♠ K 9   ♠ 8
♡ J 6   ♡ Q 8
◇ —   ◇ Q
♣ —   ♣ —

          ♠ 4
          ♡ A 3
          ◇ —
          ♣ A

thrown from dummy and East discards his spade without pain. But on the next trick the play of a spade to the ace applies the screw to East, who has to succumb in one of the red suits.

The inverted positional double squeeze is quite rigid in form. Few variations are possible, although either of the two-card menaces may be accompanied by extra winners without spoiling the position. What is not permissible is to have a winner in the suit threatening the opponent on the right at the time when the squeeze card is led. Let us track backwards from the last dia-gram and see what might happen.

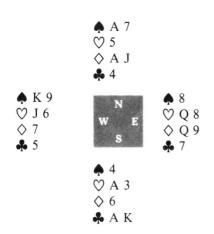

♠ A 7
♡ 5
◇ A J
♣ 4

♠ K 9   ♠ 8
♡ J 6   ♡ Q 8
◇ 7   ◇ Q 9
♣ 5   ♣ 7

♠ 4
♡ A 3
◇ 6
♣ A K

If South cashes the ace and king of clubs there is no squeeze. West discards his diamond, and South cannot find a good card to play from dummy.

To enforce the squeeze in this diagram, declarer has to play a diamond to the ace (a form of Vienna Coup) before finishing the clubs. Then every-thing falls into place.

In diagnosing this type of squeeze at the table the main problem is one of recognition. You have to know what you are looking for.

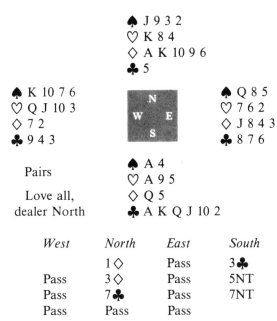

```
              ♠ J 9 3 2
              ♡ K 8 4
              ◇ A K 10 9 6
              ♣ 5

♠ K 10 7 6                      ♠ Q 8 5
♡ Q J 10 3         N            ♡ 7 6 2
◇ 7 2          W       E        ◇ J 8 4 3
♣ 9 4 3            S            ♣ 8 7 6

Pairs         ♠ A 4
              ♡ A 9 5
Love all,     ◇ Q 5
dealer North  ♣ A K Q J 10 2
```

West	North	East	South
	1◇	Pass	3♣
Pass	3◇	Pass	5NT
Pass	7♣	Pass	7NT
Pass	Pass	Pass	

You arrive in a reasonable grand slam and West leads the queen of hearts. Winning in hand with the ace, you test the diamonds by playing queen, king and ace. East follows to the third diamond but the jack has not appeared. What do you discard from hand?

If the jack of diamonds does not drop you will be a trick short and will have to fall back on a squeeze. West might have the king and queen of spades, in which case he will be caught by a simple squeeze in the majors when you run the clubs. Alternatively, East could hold both top spades. In that case he will be squeezed in spades and diamonds if you run the clubs and continue with a heart to the king.

But the most likely contingency is that the spade honours will be divided. Then your only hope will be an inverted positional double squeeze with spades as the double menace. On no account should you discard the small spade on the third round of diamonds. Keep your options open by discarding a heart, and then run the clubs. Here is the end position.

[24]

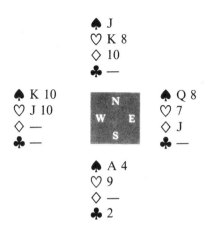

The two of clubs is played and West is the first to feel the pressure. West has to part with a spade in order to keep his heart guard, whereupon you discard the eight of hearts from the table. East has an easy discard of a heart on this trick, but when you continue with a heart to the king he is fatally squeezed in spades and diamonds.

Note the importance of testing the diamonds first on this hand. If you run the clubs immediately there is no squeeze.

At times a little preparatory work is required.

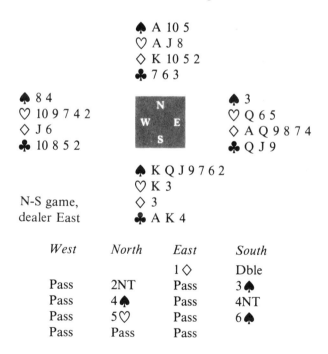

♠ A 10 5
♡ A J 8
◇ K 10 5 2
♣ 7 6 3

♠ 8 4
♡ 10 9 7 4 2
◇ J 6
♣ 10 8 5 2

♠ 3
♡ Q 6 5
◇ A Q 9 8 7 4
♣ Q J 9

♠ K Q J 9 7 6 2
♡ K 3
◇ 3
♣ A K 4

N-S game,
dealer East

West	North	East	South
		1◇	Dble
Pass	2NT	Pass	3♠
Pass	4♠	Pass	4NT
Pass	5♡	Pass	6♠
Pass	Pass	Pass	

[25]

West leads the jack of diamonds which is covered by the king and ace. East returns the queen of clubs to your ace, and you draw trumps ending in dummy. What now?

There are eleven top tricks but it is not easy to see where the twelfth might come from. The heart queen is bound to be with East, who does not have much else for his opening bid. Any attempt to squeeze East in the red suits will fail, for both menaces are on the table and dummy will have to discard ahead of East in the ending.

The only real chance is to play for an inverted double squeeze, using clubs as the double menace. For that you will need a heart menace against West. None is apparent, but you may be able to establish one by leading the jack of hearts from dummy at trick five. If West plays low you run the jack, then unblock the hearts and return to dummy in trumps to take your discard on the ace of hearts.

In practice East is sure to cover the jack of hearts, forcing you to win with the king. Now you must hope that the heart menace against West is established. Cross to dummy in trumps, ruff a diamond and then run the trumps to produce this ending.

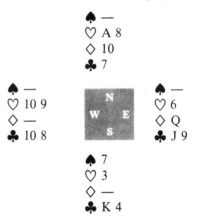

Is the pattern becoming familiar? The last spade forces West to discard a club. The eight of hearts goes from dummy while East also discards a heart. Now the play of a heart to the ace squeezes East in the minor suits and the slam is home.

SQUEEZE CARD IN OPPONENTS' SUITS

In squeeze play you normally run a long suit, the last card of which becomes the squeeze card. But there is one type of sequential double squeeze in which each defender is made to suffer by the play of a winner in his partner's suit. This is very satisfying from declarer's point of view. Here is the basic diagram.

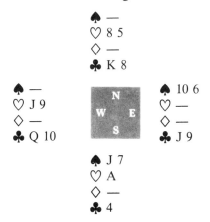

♠ —
♡ 8 5
◊ —
♣ K 8

♠ —
♡ J 9
◊ —
♣ Q 10

♠ 10 6
♡ —
◊ —
♣ J 9

♠ J 7
♡ A
◊ —
♣ 4

The position is unusual in that all three menaces are of two-card length. The arrangement of entries is such that the necessary communication is contained within a four-card diagram.

Declarer cashes the ace of hearts and East has to part with a club in order to retain his spade guard. The play of the jack of spades then squeezes West in hearts and clubs.

Strangely enough, this is a situation in which either defender can be squeezed first. If South starts with the jack of spades in the diagram, West has to part with a club. A heart is thrown from dummy, and then the play of the ace of hearts squeezes East.

Naturally a real bridge player will always cash the ace of hearts first. This enables him to check if the hearts are breaking before he has to make any embarrassing discard from dummy. In spite of the flexible arrangement of entries and menaces this is still a positional squeeze. The menaces have to lie over the threatened defenders, otherwise the squeeze will not work.

A declarer is unlikely to stumble on this sort of squeeze by accident, for he has to be aware of the advantages of blocking one of his suits in the ending. Here is the hand that gave rise to the last diagram.

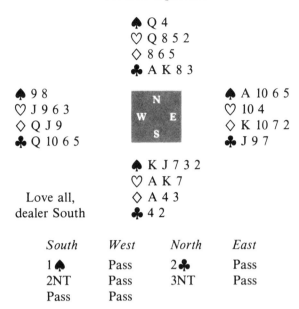

Love all,
dealer South

South	West	North	East
1 ♠	Pass	2 ♣	Pass
2NT	Pass	3NT	Pass
Pass	Pass		

An attack in hearts or clubs would have given declarer an easy time, but West led the queen of diamonds and South held up his ace until the third round. A spade went to the queen and ace, and East cashed the thirteenth diamond, South discarding a spade while West and North threw clubs. East then returned the five of spades to declarer's king.

West had echoed in spades, which seemed to indicate that the suit was not breaking. An even heart break was still a possibility, but South was not willing to rely entirely on this. Seeing a chance of a sequential double squeeze ending, he played a club to the ace, cashed the queen of hearts and continued with a heart to his king to achieve the position shown in

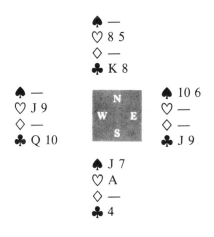

the diagram. The ace of hearts ruined East, after which the jack of spades applied the *coup de grace* to West.

The declarer played well, but East was in rather too much of a hurry to take his tricks. If he had ducked twice in spades, or if he had won the ace and returned the suit without cashing his diamond, the timing would have been wrong for declarer and the squeeze would have come to naught.

A defensive slip is also a feature of the next hand, which comes from the 1982 World Pairs Olympiad in Biarritz.

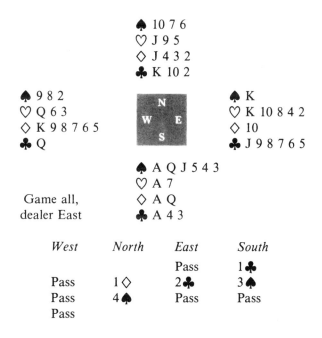

West	North	East	South
		Pass	1♣
Pass	1♦	2♣	3♠
Pass	4♠	Pass	Pass
Pass			

After a strong club, a negative response and an intervention in clubs, South rebid three spades. North raised to game in spades and West led the queen of clubs.

Declarer might have won on the table in order to take a spade finesse, but he thought it might be useful to preserve dummy's entry for later. He therefore won the first trick in hand with the ace of clubs and cashed the spade ace, receiving his reward when the king dropped. Two more rounds of spades were followed by a diamond to the queen and king. West returned a diamond to the ace, and declarer played three more rounds of trumps to reach the diagram position.

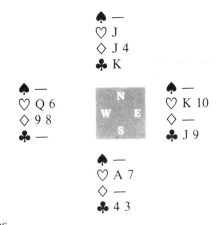

♠ —
♡ J
♢ J 4
♣ K

♠ —
♡ Q 6
♢ 9 8
♣ —

♠ —
♡ K 10
♢ —
♣ J 9

♠ —
♡ A 7
♢ —
♣ 4 3

West was known to have the diamonds and East the clubs, so the double squeeze was sure to deliver the goods. The play of a club to the king forced West to discard a heart, after which the jack of diamonds squeezed East in hearts and clubs.

Making twelve tricks in spades produced an undisputed top for North and South.

Do you see how the defence could have done better? When in with the king of diamonds, West might have switched to a heart. This takes out the entry in the double-menace suit and kills off all squeeze possibilities.

An attack on the double menace is often the right move for the defenders. We shall look more closely at this in a later chapter.

2

The Automatic Double Squeeze

A squeeze will function automatically only if there is an idle card in the hand opposite the squeeze card which can be discarded irrespective of the actions of the defenders. For the double squeeze this translates into a requirement that the double menace must be of at least three cards in length. Here is the basic matrix for the automatic double squeeze.

In this four-card ending both one-card menaces are in the same hand as the squeeze card and the double menace is in the opposite hand. Note that the hand containing the squeeze card holds only one card in the double-menace suit. This is necessary in order to allow space for the other menaces.

When the ace of clubs is played each defender is squeezed automatically. West has to re-

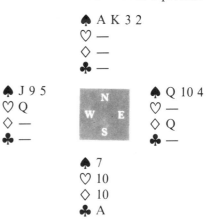

tain his heart and East his diamond, and neither can hang on to three spades.

Not much is permissible in the way of variation in the above diagram, although dummy's idle spade could be replaced by a card in any of the other three suits. Also, either of the one-card menaces may be accompanied by a winner without harming the prospects. This produces a sequential, rather than a simultaneous, squeeze.

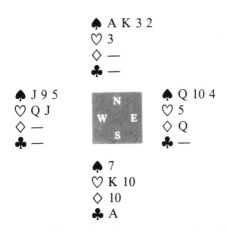

In this five-card ending a winner has been added to the one-card menace against West. The ace of clubs squeezes West, who has to part with a spade. At the next trick the play of the king of hearts squeezes East in diamonds and spades.

But there is no special merit in this sequence of play. It is better to avoid all ambiguity by cashing the king of hearts first. Then the play of the ace of clubs inflicts the simultaneous double squeeze.

Similarly, if we add a winner to the single menace against East we can arrive at the position shown in the new diagram.

On the play of the ace of clubs West can throw his diamond, but East is squeezed and has to part with a spade. Now the king of diamonds squeezes West in the major suits.

As in the previous case, it is better to reduce to the simultaneous position by cashing the king of diamonds first.

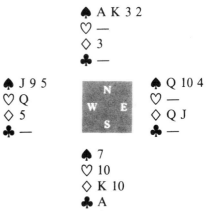

The automatic double squeeze, with its requirement of a three-card double menace opposite a singleton, is quite rigid in structure. This very fact makes it easy to recognise, and it is just as easy to play. Here is an example.

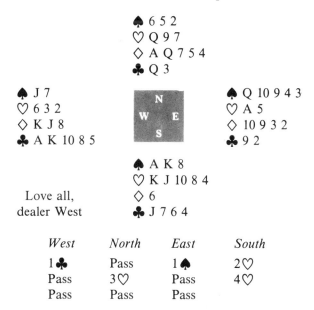

```
                    ♠ 6 5 2
                    ♡ Q 9 7
                    ◇ A Q 7 5 4
                    ♣ Q 3
    ♠ J 7                           ♠ Q 10 9 4 3
    ♡ 6 3 2              N          ♡ A 5
    ◇ K J 8          W       E      ◇ 10 9 3 2
    ♣ A K 10 8 5         S          ♣ 9 2
                    ♠ A K 8
                    ♡ K J 10 8 4
    Love all,        ◇ 6
    dealer West      ♣ J 7 6 4
```

West	North	East	South
1♣	Pass	1♠	2♡
Pass	3♡	Pass	4♡
Pass	Pass	Pass	

The opening lead is the ace of clubs on which East plays the nine. West switches smartly to a trump, East taking the ace and continuing with a second trump. You play the queen of clubs to knock out the ace and West perseveres with a third trump, East discarding a spade.

The defenders have denied you a club ruff in dummy, but does it really matter? At this stage the hand is an open book. West is marked with five clubs and he must surely have the king of diamonds to account for his opening bid. You can be certain that East began with five spades, for otherwise his response would have been one diamond. So you can count nine tricks with the help of the diamond finesse, and you have spade and club menaces in hand. The automatic double squeeze is bound to provide the tenth trick.

Just cash the top spades and the jack of clubs, and then apply pressure with the trumps.

Here is the end position:

On the play of the jack of hearts both defenders have to throw diamonds. Now you finesse the queen of diamonds, cash the ace and take the last trick with the diamond seven.

It was entirely natural for West to lead a top club, but in practice this cost a vital tempo. If the defence starts with two rounds of trumps, West can play a third trump when he first

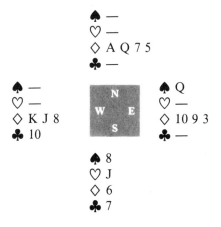

gains the lead in clubs. Then, when in with the second club, he can switch to a diamond, neutralising the double menace and killing all chance of a squeeze.

SIMPLE SQUEEZE PLAYED AS DOUBLE

A four-card menace can threaten both defenders but only when it is opposite a singleton, as in this diagram.

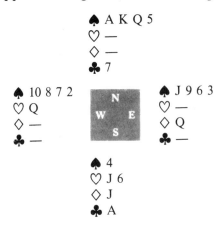

Declarer plays the ace of clubs and both defenders are squeezed automatically.

This situation does not arise with any great frequency. More often than not, declarer will have two cards in the suit of the four-card menace, in which case no double squeeze can be present since only one of the defenders can guard the suit. But the four-card menace can still be of some value. A common position is shown in the next diagram.

Technically there is no double squeeze, since only one of the defenders can guard the hearts.

But does declarer care, knowing that he has a spade menace against West and a club menace against East? Of course not! The *form* of the double squeeze is there, and declarer simply plays the last diamond, knowing that he is bound to flatten the defender who controls the hearts.

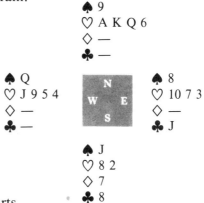

♠ 9
♡ A K Q 6
◇ —
♣ —

♠ Q   ♠ 8
♡ J 9 5 4   ♡ 10 7 3
◇ —   ◇ —
♣ —   ♣ J

♠ J
♡ 8 2
◇ 7
♣ 8

This is sometimes called the 'Either-Or' squeeze. Declarer knows that he will squeeze either East or West, depending on who has the long hearts. Here is the hand that gave rise to the last ending.

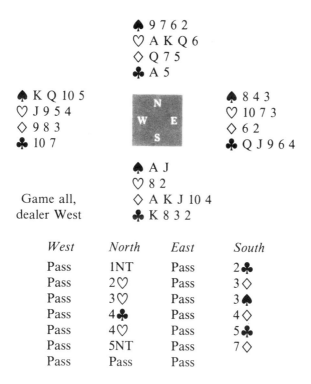

♠ 9 7 6 2
♡ A K Q 6
◇ Q 7 5
♣ A 5

♠ K Q 10 5   ♠ 8 4 3
♡ J 9 5 4   ♡ 10 7 3
◇ 9 8 3   ◇ 6 2
♣ 10 7   ♣ Q J 9 6 4

♠ A J
♡ 8 2
◇ A K J 10 4
♣ K 8 3 2

Game all,
dealer West

West	North	East	South
Pass	1NT	Pass	2♣
Pass	2♡	Pass	3◇
Pass	3♡	Pass	3♠
Pass	4♣	Pass	4◇
Pass	4♡	Pass	5♣
Pass	5NT	Pass	7◇
Pass	Pass	Pass	

West leads the king of spades against the grand slam. Declarer wins with the ace and plays on clubs. West ruffs the third club with the eight of diamonds and, after over-ruffing with the queen, South returns to hand with a trump.

It would be dangerous to try to ruff another club, and it is quite unnecessary. Declarer has a spade menace against West and a club menace against East. Hence neither of them will be able to hold four hearts when the trumps are run. As it happens it is West who is caught in a major-suit squeeze. But if West had started with a spade more and a heart fewer, East would have been squeezed in hearts and clubs.

This sort of situation comes up often enough to be worth remembering. A knowledge of double squeeze technique will enable you to execute a number of simple squeezes that might otherwise escape. When the conditions are right, play the hand as a double squeeze, but don't be surprised if you find you have squeezed only one of the opponents. The double menace does not have to be of four-card length and the squeeze need not be automatic. The diagram shows a positional ending.

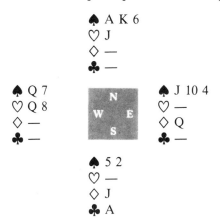

♠ A K 6
♡ J
◇ —
♣ —

♠ Q 7   ♠ J 10 4
♡ Q 8   ♡ —
◇ —   ◇ Q
♣ —   ♣ —

♠ 5 2
♡ —
◇ J
♣ A

Knowing you have a heart menace against West and a diamond menace against East, you aim for a positional double squeeze. But it may be that West started with a doubleton spade, in which case it is only East who can be squeezed. Never mind. All is grist to the mill. You don't care whether you squeeze one opponent or two as long as the extra trick rolls in.

The split three-card menace, useful in so many forms of squeeze play, has no role to play in the double automatic squeeze. This is due to the natural limitations of space. A double squeeze involving a split three-card menace is always positional in character. However, a split four-card menace can provide the form, if not the substance, of an automatic double squeeze.

There can be no true double squeeze in the diagram position, but the machinery is in place and that is what counts. If the red queens in dummy menace separate opponents, nobody will be able to hold four spades when the ace of clubs is played.

The diagram illustrates an inverted form of the 'Either-

♠ K 5
♡ Q
◇ Q
♣ 7

♠ A Q 7 4
♡ —
◇ —
♣ A

Or' squeeze, but the split four-card menace can be just as effective when the length is opposite the squeeze card. Here is an example.

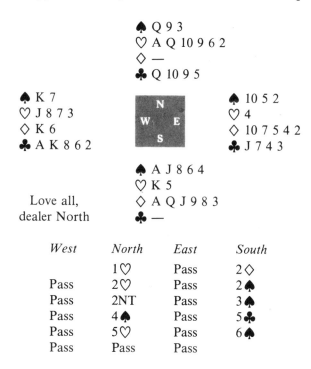

♠ Q 9 3
♡ A Q 10 9 6 2
◇ —
♣ Q 10 9 5

♠ K 7
♡ J 8 7 3
◇ K 6
♣ A K 8 6 2

♠ 10 5 2
♡ 4
◇ 10 7 5 4 2
♣ J 7 4 3

♠ A J 8 6 4
♡ K 5
◇ A Q J 9 8 3
♣ —

Love all,
dealer North

West	North	East	South
	1♡	Pass	2◇
Pass	2♡	Pass	2♠
Pass	2NT	Pass	3♠
Pass	4♠	Pass	5♣
Pass	5♡	Pass	6♠
Pass	Pass	Pass	

[37]

South trumped the opening lead of the king of clubs, ruffed a small diamond in dummy and ran the queen of spades, losing to the king. West returned his trump and declarer drew a third round. Avoiding the trap of testing the hearts prematurely, South cashed the ace of diamonds and received a bonus when the king fell. On the queen and jack of diamonds West discarded his remaining small clubs, but the play of the last trump in the diagram position turned the screw. Unable to keep four hearts and the ace of clubs, West had to surrender.

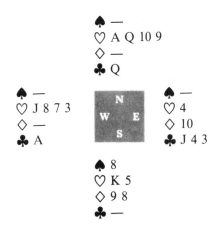

If East had held the heart guard, he would have been squeezed in the red suits and the slam would still have been made.

With the club menace sitting over West, this was in fact a positional squeeze. But the form was automatic. If South had held the club menace instead of the eight of diamonds in the diagram, the squeeze would have worked equally well.

A point of defence is worth noting. An initial heart lead would have given the defenders a flying start, for when in with the king of spades West would have been able to give his partner a heart ruff. This defence is difficult but not impossible for West to find. On the bidding South is clearly marked with a 5-2-6-0 shape, and West has only to visualise six hearts on his left to see the possibilities.

INVERSION

The true inverted form of the automatic double squeeze, where there is no entry opposite the squeeze card in the suit of the long menace, is a sequential rather than a simultaneous position. The form is rigid, with little in the way of variation being allowable. Here is the basic matrix.

When the ace of clubs is played, West discards a diamond while a spade is thrown from the table. East feels the pressure first and has to part with a spade. Now the play of a diamond to the ace squeezes West in the major suits.

As always in the case of the automatic double squeeze, the double menace must be of three-card length. That is the main frailty of this type of squeeze. If

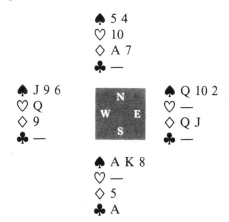

♠ 5 4
♡ 10
◇ A 7
♣ —

♠ J 9 6
♡ Q
◇ 9
♣ —

♠ Q 10 2
♡ —
◇ Q J
♣ —

♠ A K 8
♡ —
◇ 5
♣ A

the defenders had been able to play a round of spades at an earlier stage, the squeeze would have failed for the simple reason that declarer would have had no idle card in dummy to discard on the ace of clubs.

This opens up great vistas in defence and we shall deal fully with the possibilities in a later chapter. Sometimes the defenders have no option but to go quietly, as in the following example.

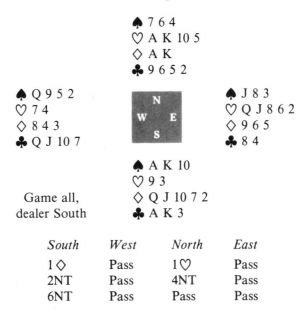

```
            ♠ 7 6 4
            ♡ A K 10 5
            ◇ A K
            ♣ 9 6 5 2
♠ Q 9 5 2           N        ♠ J 8 3
♡ 7 4        W            E  ♡ Q J 8 6 2
◇ 8 4 3             S        ◇ 9 6 5
♣ Q J 10 7                   ♣ 8 4
            ♠ A K 10
            ♡ 9 3
Game all,   ◇ Q J 10 7 2
dealer South ♣ A K 3
```

South	West	North	East
1 ◇	Pass	1 ♡	Pass
2NT	Pass	4NT	Pass
6NT	Pass	Pass	Pass

Bidding aggressively on the strength of their good controls, North and South reach a contract of six no-trumps and West makes the natural lead of the queen of clubs.

Since South can count eleven top tricks, he holds off at trick one to rectify the count for a possible squeeze. West may continue clubs or switch to a heart, but the hand practically plays itself. Declarer unblocks the diamonds, tests the clubs and runs the rest of the diamonds to reach this ending:

When the ten of diamonds is played West discards a heart and dummy a spade. East comes under heavy pressure and has to part with a spade. Now the play of a heart to the king squeezes West in the black suits and the slam is made.

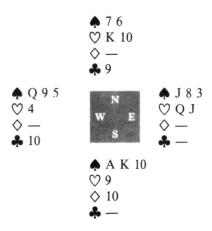

```
            ♠ 7 6
            ♡ K 10
            ◇ —
            ♣ 9
♠ Q 9 5            N        ♠ J 8 3
♡ 4          W           E  ♡ Q J
◇ —                S        ◇ —
♣ 10                        ♣ —
            ♠ A K 10
            ♡ 9
            ◇ 10
            ♣ —
```

West might have thought of attacking the double menace by switching to a spade at trick two, but on the lie of the cards this defence is ineffective. If West leads a low spade to the jack and king, he exposes himself to a simple squeeze in the black suits when declarer runs the diamonds, cashes the clubs and plays off the hearts. And if West tries a switch to the queen of spades, his partner is subjected to an automatic squeeze in the majors when declarer cashes his minor-suit winners. South need not consider a second-round spade finesse.

The only defence that works is for West to lead a heart initially, and that is perhaps too hard to find.

PRESERVING THE LONG MENACE

The main danger in automatic double squeeze play may come not from the defenders but from declarer himself. The temptation to reduce the double menace to two cards in length is sometimes very strong.

```
                        ♠ A K 8 5
                        ♡ 7 6 4 3
                        ◇ 8 7 6 2
                        ♣ Q
        ♠ 9 7                             ♠ Q J 10 6 3
        ♡ J 9 5                           ♡ K 10 2
        ◇ A K Q 10 9 4                    ◇ J 5
        ♣ J 6                             ♣ 10 8 4
                        ♠ 4 2
                        ♡ A Q 8
  Love all,            ◇ 3
  dealer West          ♣ A K 9 7 5 3 2
```

West	North	East	South
1 ◇	Pass	1 ♠	3 ♣
Pass	4 ♣	Pass	4 ♡
Pass	4 ♠	Pass	6 ♣
Pass	Pass	Pass	

Pressing hard once again, South reaches a shaky slam in clubs. West attacks in diamonds and South ruffs the second round. Both defenders follow when a club is played to the queen, and declarer is at the cross-roads.

Clearly he needs the heart finesse to be right. There could be a simple squeeze for the twelfth trick if either defender has four hearts, but this must be unlikely. The alternative is an inverted double squeeze, and declarer may be tempted to finesse the queen of hearts at trick four and then run the trumps. But the positional double squeeze cannot work since dummy has no entry in West's suit. The only double squeeze available is the automatic one, and for that the double menace in hearts must be preserved.

Declarer must return to hand with a diamond ruff in spite of the risk of an uppercut from East. As it happens East can do no damage, and the trumps are run to produce this ending:

On the play of the nine of clubs West discards a spade, a heart is thrown from dummy and East reluctantly parts with a heart. The play of the top spades then squeezes West in the red suits, and the slam is made with the help of the heart finesse.

Clearly the slam would have been defeated if West had found

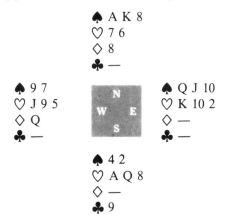

♠ A K 8
♡ 7 6
◇ 8
♣ —

♠ 9 7   ♠ Q J 10
♡ J 9 5   ♡ K 10 2
◇ Q   ◇ —
♣ —   ♣ —

♠ 4 2
♡ A Q 8
◇ —
♣ 9

the inspiration to switch to a heart at trick two, or if he had led either major suit at trick one. Fortunately for declarers, few players are capable of producing such defences.

VARIATIONS

As noted before, the inverted type of double automatic squeeze is quite rigid in form. The three-card double menace has to be in the same hand as the squeeze card, and in the opposite hand there must be a two-card menace against the opponent on the right of the squeeze card. The other

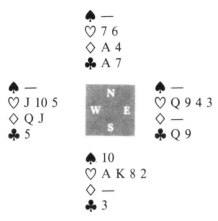

♠ —
♡ 7 6
♢ A 4
♣ A 7

♠ —
♡ J 10 5
♢ Q J
♣ 5

♠ —
♡ Q 9 4 3
♢ —
♣ Q 9

♠ 10
♡ A K 8 2
♢ —
♣ 3

menace may also be accompanied by a winner, however, without spoiling the force of the squeeze.

In this six-card ending the defenders are under no pressure when the ten of spades is led. West discards his club while dummy and East throw hearts. But when the three of clubs is led to the next trick West has to part with a heart in order to keep his diamond guard. The ace of clubs wins, and the ace of diamonds squeezes East at the next trick.

This automatic ending is analagous to the positional squeeze we saw on page 28, where each defender is squeezed by the play of the master card in his partner's suit. Here is the sort of hand on which the ending might arise.

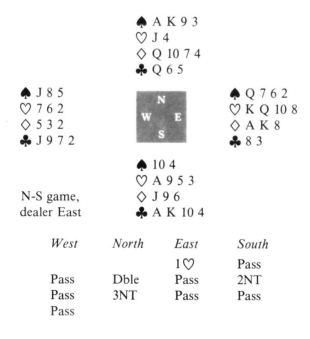

♠ A K 9 3
♡ J 4
♢ Q 10 7 4
♣ Q 6 5

♠ J 8 5
♡ 7 6 2
♢ 5 3 2
♣ J 9 7 2

♠ Q 7 6 2
♡ K Q 10 8
♢ A K 8
♣ 8 3

♠ 10 4
♡ A 9 5 3
♢ J 9 6
♣ A K 10 4

N-S game,
dealer East

West	North	East	South
		1 ♡	Pass
Pass	Dble	Pass	2NT
Pass	3NT	Pass	Pass
Pass			

West leads the seven of hearts to the four, ten and three. East continues with the king of hearts which again wins the trick. Next comes a switch to the eight of clubs. How do you plan the play?

After knocking out the top diamonds you will have eight tricks, but on this switch it looks as though West has the clubs guarded. The chances of a double spade finesse must be small; East is likely to have something in spades for his opening bid.

What are the squeeze chances? You appear to have a club menace against West and a heart menace against East, and spades will serve as the long menace for a double squeeze. The last free winner will be the fourth diamond, which is in the same hand as the long menace, so it is the inverted form of automatic double squeeze you have to aim for. Win the club with the ace and run the diamond nine to the king. Win the next club with the queen and con-tinue with a low diamond from dummy. East cannot hold off without suffering an end-play at the next trick, so he will win and return the suit. You over-take the jack of diamonds with the queen and continue with the ten of diamonds in this position:

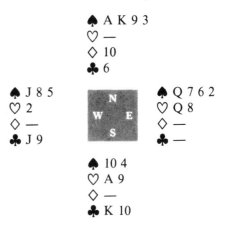

```
                    ♠ A K 9 3
                    ♡ —
                    ◇ 10
                    ♣ 6
♠ J 8 5                           ♠ Q 7 6 2
♡ 2           N                   ♡ Q 8
◇ —        W     E                ◇ —
♣ J 9         S                   ♣ —
                    ♠ 10 4
                    ♡ A 9
                    ◇ —
                    ♣ K 10
```

East discards a spade, so do you, and West throws his idle heart. But on the next play of the six of clubs East has to part with another spade. The king of clubs wins, and the heart ace gives West a headache in the black suits.

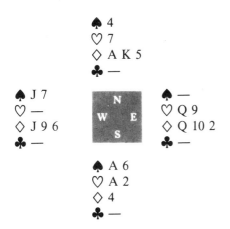

♠ 4
♡ 7
◇ A K 5
♣ —

♠ J 7
♡ —
◇ J 9 6
♣ —

♠ —
♡ Q 9
◇ Q 10 2
♣ —

♠ A 6
♡ A 2
◇ 4
♣ —

In these automatic endings where there is no separate squeeze card, either defender may be squeezed first if there is communication in every suit.

If South plays the ace of spades East is squeezed first in the red suits, after which the play of the ace of hearts squeezes West in spades and diamonds.

Alternatively, South may start with the ace of hearts, squeezing West first. The play of the ace of spades then applies pressure to East.

Such positions are not too common, but when they do turn up the hand usually plays itself.

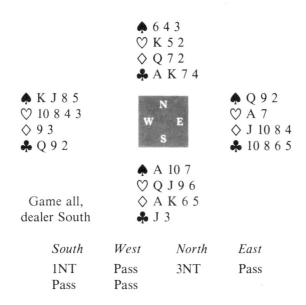

♠ 6 4 3
♡ K 5 2
◇ Q 7 2
♣ A K 7 4

♠ K J 8 5
♡ 10 8 4 3
◇ 9 3
♣ Q 9 2

♠ Q 9 2
♡ A 7
◇ J 10 8 4
♣ 10 8 6 5

♠ A 10 7
♡ Q J 9 6
◇ A K 6 5
♣ J 3

Game all,
dealer South

South	West	North	East
1NT	Pass	3NT	Pass
Pass	Pass		

West leads the five of spades to his partner's queen. You hold off at trick one but win the second spade with the ace and play the six of hearts to the king and ace. East returns his spade and West cashes the fourth round, on which everyone discards clubs. This is the position:

A switch to the queen of clubs at this point would leave you with no chance, but fortunately West is unable to see through the back of the cards. He returns the nine of diamonds which you win with dummy's queen.

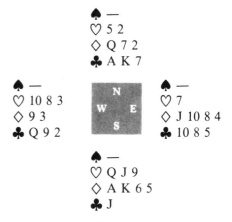

♠ —
♡ 5 2
◇ Q 7 2
♣ A K 7

♠ —
♡ 10 8 3
◇ 9 3
♣ Q 9 2

♠ —
♡ 7
◇ J 10 8 4
♣ 10 8 5

♠ —
♡ Q J 9
◇ A K 6 5
♣ J

There is nothing to do but test the red suits. You may cash the queen and jack of hearts, squeezing East in the minors, and then play off the top diamonds to squeeze West, or you may do it the other way round. In either case the result is nine tricks.

3

The Double Ruffing Squeeze

Most double squeezes involve three menaces, as we have seen. Each defender is menaced separately in a suit that only he can guard, and both come under pressure in a third suit.

In the double ruffing squeeze, however, both defenders are squeezed in the same two suits. This requires two double menaces, one of which is a normal split menace. The other is a ruffing menace of a special type. Consider the layout of the spade suit in this diagram.

The position is such that neither defender can part with a spade without loss. If East throws a spade, declarer plays the jack from dummy and ruffs out the ace. If West throws a spade, the play of the king from dummy allows the ace to be ruffed out as the queen is pinned.

So when the ace of clubs is played in the diagram position both defenders have to discard

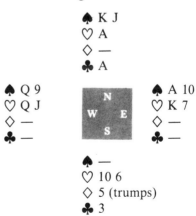

hearts. This suits declarer just as well. He cashes the ace of hearts and then ruffs himself back to hand to enjoy the established heart ten.

Note that the pressure is applied on the play of the *second-last* free winner. Declarer must have a trump left after the squeeze has taken effect, otherwise the ruffing option is lost.

All ruffing squeezes require two cards of entry in the hand that contains the ruffing menace—one to establish the menace and the other to cash it. One of these entries must be a master card in the suit of the split menace; the other may lie in any of the three side suits. When the second entry is in the free suit, as in the last diagram, it will also be the squeeze card.

You may remember that, in the case of the simple ruffing squeeze, the second entry may lie in the trump suit. This applies in theory to the double ruffing squeeze as well, but in practice it results in a ridiculous ending.

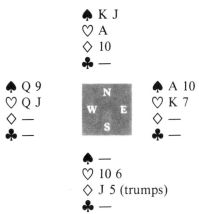

Dummy has one entry in hearts and another in trumps. If South insists on doing things the hard way, he can play the five of diamonds to dummy's ten to inflict the double ruffing squeeze.

But this is quite unnecessary. In the double ruffing squeeze *both* defenders have to come under pressure. For the squeeze to work in this diagram, neither of them can have a trump left when a diamond is played to the ten. No squeeze is therefore required. A sensible declarer will make *sure* of four tricks by cross-ruffing.

The second entry to dummy is often provided by an extension to the split menace, as is shown in the next diagram.

Declarer has a split three-card menace in hearts, dummy holding an extra master card in the suit.

This is a common layout and the double ruffing squeeze works like a charm. When the ace of clubs is played West cannot afford to throw a spade and must therefore part with a heart. The seven of hearts is thrown from the table and East faces the same dilemma. When

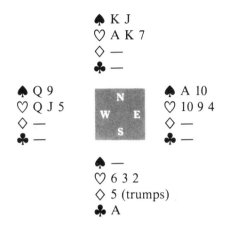

he also discards a heart, declarer cashes the top hearts to make his hand high.

There is no need for the ruffing menace to take the precise form shown in the previous diagrams. Extend the ruffing menace by giving dummy a

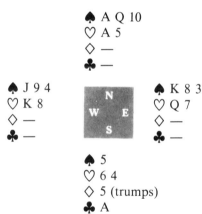

master card in the suit and we have a third way of meeting the entry requirements.

South plays the ace of clubs, discarding the five of hearts from the table. If either defender parts with a spade, South continues with a spade to the ace and establishes a second spade trick with a ruff.

The defenders are no better off if they both discard hearts. A heart to the ace is followed by the ace of spades and a spade ruff, and South scores the last trick with his established heart.

The double ruffing squeeze is not a play that will be encountered every day—or even every week, month or year. For all that, it is worth storing in a pigeon-hole of the memory. When an opportunity does arise, the position is easily recognised because of the special nature of the ruffing menace.

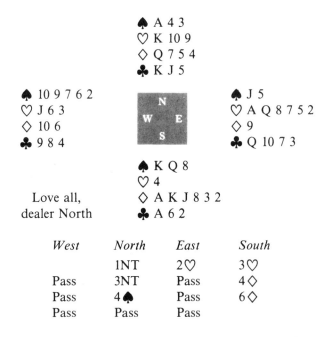

```
                    ♠ A 4 3
                    ♡ K 10 9
                    ◇ Q 7 5 4
                    ♣ K J 5
 ♠ 10 9 7 6 2                        ♠ J 5
 ♡ J 6 3                             ♡ A Q 8 7 5 2
 ◇ 10 6                              ◇ 9
 ♣ 9 8 4                             ♣ Q 10 7 3
                    ♠ K Q 8
                    ♡ 4
  Love all,         ◇ A K J 8 3 2
  dealer North      ♣ A 6 2
```

West	North	East	South
	1NT	2♡	3♡
Pass	3NT	Pass	4◇
Pass	4♠	Pass	6◇
Pass	Pass	Pass	

West leads the three of hearts to the nine and queen, and East switches to his trump. How do you plan the play?

There are only eleven tricks in immediate view and the club finesse does not look like a good bet. However, there is an interesting position in hearts. Unless both defenders have false-carded, it looks as though West has the jack of hearts. In that case you can forget about the club finesse, for a double ruffing squeeze will make a certainty of the contract.

The Double Ruffing Squeeze

Ruffing squeezes often suffer from a built-in defect. Ambiguity is likely to be present unless you have an accurate count of one of the key suits. In this case you can be fairly sure that East will have six hearts for his two-level overcall, and you can hardly go wrong in the ending. Just play five rounds of diamonds, discarding a club from the table, and play off the king queen of spades. This will be the position:

When you continue with a spade to the ace, neither defender will be able to discard a heart without conceding your twelfth trick in that suit. The alternative is for them both to throw clubs, but this serves the defensive cause no better. You cash the king of clubs and

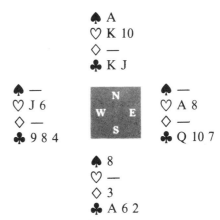

continue with the jack to the queen and ace, scoring your twelfth trick with the established six of clubs.

The above ending was a little unusual in that declarer's communications were augmented in the club suit. The three-card split menace with master cards in each hand meant that declarer had no need to ruff himself back to hand. But the ruffing option was needed in case either defender discarded a heart. And the extra line of communication in clubs was by no means essential. The squeeze works just as well if, in the diagram position, South cashes the ace of clubs before playing his spade to the ace.

More usually declarer will have no communication with his own hand after the squeeze has taken place apart from that essential last trump. Try your hand at a grand slam.

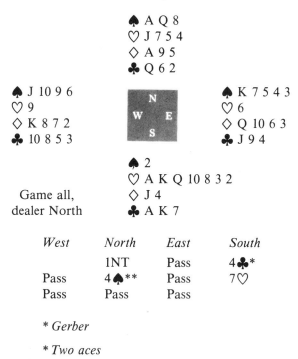

♠ A Q 8
♡ J 7 5 4
◇ A 9 5
♣ Q 6 2

♠ J 10 9 6
♡ 9
◇ K 8 7 2
♣ 10 8 5 3

♠ K 7 5 4 3
♡ 6
◇ Q 10 6 3
♣ J 9 4

♠ 2
♡ A K Q 10 8 3 2
◇ J 4
♣ A K 7

Game all,
dealer North

West	North	East	South
	1NT	Pass	4♣*
Pass	4♠**	Pass	7♡
Pass	Pass	Pass	

* *Gerber*

* *Two aces*

West leads the jack of spades. How do you plan the play?

Not many defenders lead away from kings against grand slams, so you have little option but to play the ace of spades at trick one. That leaves you looking at what appears to be an unavoidable loser in diamonds. However, the spades remaining in dummy may suggest the possibility of a double ruffing squeeze. You have a split two-card menace in diamonds, and the diamond ace and the club queen will serve as the two entries to dummy that are needed for the ending.

The hand virtually plays itself. Just run six rounds of trumps, discarding two diamonds from the table, and then cash the ace and king

[52]

of clubs. The position is as shown in the diagram.

You have to hope that West has both the ten and the nine of spades in this ending. When you continue with the seven of clubs to dummy's queen the defenders are caught in the familiar dilemma. If either of them discards a spade, you can set up your thirteenth trick in that suit. If both defenders throw diamonds, the jack of diamonds is established in your hand.

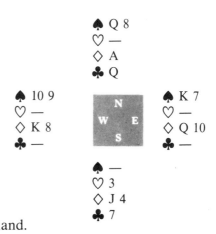

♠ Q 8
♡ —
◇ A
♣ Q

♠ 10 9   ♠ K 7
♡ —   ♡ —
◇ K 8   ◇ Q 10
♣ —   ♣ —

♠ —
♡ 3
◇ J 4
♣ 7

But note the element of ambiguity that is often present in such positions. Clever defenders might attempt to deceive you by keeping different cards for the four-card ending, as is shown in the new diagram.

East has already bared his king of spades and West his king of diamonds. If West now discards the nine of spades and East a diamond on your club lead, you will probably go astray by leading the queen of spades from dummy.

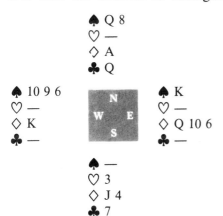

♠ Q 8
♡ —
◇ A
♣ Q

♠ 10 9 6   ♠ K
♡ —   ♡ —
◇ K   ◇ Q 10 6
♣ —   ♣ —

♠ —
♡ 3
◇ J 4
♣ 7

Well, there's not much to be done about that. Accurate card-reading is the only answer to deceptive discarding.

[53]

There are a couple of other points about the defence which are worth considering. East did well in the bidding by keeping silent over four spades, for a double would have given away the position of the king. But West undid the good work when he chose the jack of spades as his opening lead. West could hardly be expected to find the killing lead of a diamond, but the trump would have been a sensible choice. It is not without good reason that a trump is recommended as the safest lead against a grand slam.

You would have to be able to see through the backs of the cards to make the slam after a trump lead. The natural line of play is to try to dispose of the diamond loser by taking a simple finesse in spades.

A TWO-LOSER SQUEEZE

Most double squeezes operate only at the direct (or one-loser) level. Declarer must be in a position to take all the tricks but one at the time when the squeeze card is led. With more than one loser, as we have seen in earlier chapters, declarer must concede a trick in the early stages in order to rectify the count.

The double ruffing squeeze is an exception to this rule for it will sometimes work perfectly well when declarer has two losers. This is made possible by the fact that the squeeze operates on the play of the *second-last* free winner, obliging the defenders to keep extended guards in the same two suits.

Anyone who fails to appreciate this point may go wrong on a hand like the following.

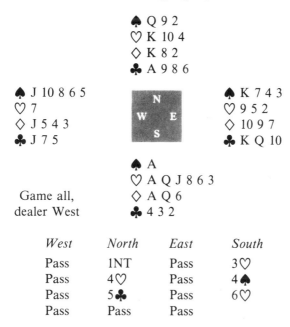

♠ Q 9 2
♡ K 10 4
◇ K 8 2
♣ A 9 8 6

♠ J 10 8 6 5
♡ 7
◇ J 5 4 3
♣ J 7 5

♠ K 7 4 3
♡ 9 5 2
◇ 10 9 7
♣ K Q 10

♠ A
♡ A Q J 8 6 3
◇ A Q 6
♣ 4 3 2

Game all,
dealer West

West	North	East	South
Pass	1NT	Pass	3♡
Pass	4♡	Pass	4♠
Pass	5♣	Pass	6♡
Pass	Pass	Pass	

You land in six hearts and again West makes the helpful lead of the jack of spades. This time it is fair to say that he had no attractive alternative, although East might with advantage have doubled five clubs. You play low from dummy and win the first trick with the ace of spades. How do you propose to make the slam?

The spade holding in dummy suggests the possibility of a double ruffing squeeze. At present you have eleven top tricks and two losers, and after drawing trumps you may consider ducking a club in order to rectify the count. But this plan has a serious defect. If you duck a club East is likely to continue the suit, taking out a vital entry to dummy before you are ready to use it and thus killing all squeeze possibilities.

There is no need to rectify the count on this hand since the double ruffing squeeze will work perfectly well with two losers. Just play five rounds of trumps, discarding two clubs from the table, and cash the ace

[55]

and queen of diamonds to reach this position:

When you continue with the six of diamonds to the king, the defenders are sunk without trace. If either of them discards a spade, you can establish a spade trick in the now-familiar way. If both discard clubs, you continue with the ace and nine of clubs to set up your twelfth trick in that suit.

Naturally there could be

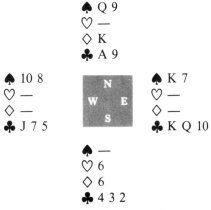

some ambiguity in the ending. You have to read the discards accurately to ensure success.

TWO RUFFING MENACES

Another type of double ruffing squeeze makes use of two ruffing menaces, only one of which need be of the special sort. The menaces are

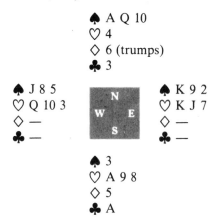

divided and there is a trump left in both hands.

In the diagram South has five winners—the three aces plus a trump in each hand. When the ace of clubs is played both defenders are squeezed in the majors and a sixth trick emerges.

This arrangement of menaces is quite flexible. The special menace may lie in either hand, as may the squeeze card. The

[56]

position can be simplified by reducing to five cards, since the menace lying in the same hand as the squeeze card need not be accompanied by a winner.

The ace of spades has been played off and the squeeze still works, but now the squeeze card has to be in the North hand. There must always be some means of communication with the ruffing menace that lies *opposite* the squeeze card.

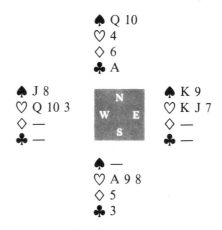

♠ Q 10
♡ 4
◇ 6
♣ A

♠ J 8
♡ Q 10 3
◇ —
♣ —

♠ K 9
♡ K J 7
◇ —
♣ —

♠ —
♡ A 9 8
◇ 5
♣ 3

This type of double ruffing squeeze is not hard to recognise when it makes an appearance.

♠ Q 10 8 4
♡ J 9 3
◇ A J 10 4 3
♣ 6

♠ 5 2
♡ A 10 6 2
◇ 9 7 5
♣ Q 9 4 3

♠ A K 3
♡ Q 8 7 5 4
◇ 8 2
♣ K J 7

♠ J 9 7 6
♡ K
◇ K Q 6
♣ A 10 8 5 2

N-S game,
dealer North

West	North	East	South
	Pass	1♡	Dble
3♡	Dble	Pass	3♠
Pass	4♠	Pass	Pass
Pass			

[57]

West leads the ace of hearts, felling your king, and switches smartly to a trump. East takes the ace and king and continues with a third round of trumps, West discarding the two of hearts. What are your prospects?

The trump leads have reduced your ruffing potential and you can count no more than nine tricks—three trumps, five diamonds and the ace of clubs. But if you look more closely you will see that the hand is tailor-made for a double ruffing squeeze. It is reasonable to hope that West has the ten of hearts and East the queen, in which case neither defender will be able to hold three clubs in the end-game. Just run the diamonds to reach the position shown in the diagram.

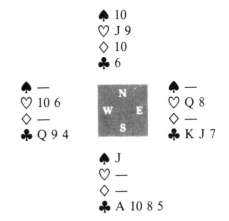

There is no fear of ambiguity in this case, for you have a good indication that East started with five hearts and West with four. Neither opponent can afford to part with a heart when the last diamond is played, and you know what to do when they both throw clubs. After a club to the ace and a club ruff, you return to hand with a heart ruff to enjoy the established ten of clubs.

After the opening lead of the ace of hearts the defenders had no way of defeating your contract. If they had started with three rounds of trumps your task would have been too difficult. West, when in with the ace of hearts, would have been able to knock out the ace of clubs, destroying all squeeze chances.

4

Wayward Forms

It is time for a brief look at those double squeezes which do not conform to the usual rules. It is not only in the double ruffing squeeze that both defenders can be squeezed in the same two suits. The miracle can be performed at no-trumps when the conditions are right.

THE DOUBLE TWO-SUIT SQUEEZE

This requires two double menaces, one a split menace and the other a three-card menace of a special type. As in the double ruffing squeeze, neither opponent is free to discard from the suit except at the cost of a trick. Here is the basic matrix.

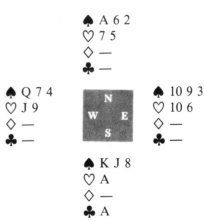

The lead of the ace of clubs squeezes West, who must part with a heart in order to keep his spade guard. The two of spades is thrown from the table and East comes under similar pressure. If he parts with a spade declarer can play the jack of spades, running it when West plays low. If West covers, the ace wins and South scores two more spade tricks in his hand.

The alternative for East is to discard a heart, in which case South cashes the ace of hearts, crosses to the ace of spades and scores an extra trick with the established seven of hearts.

Declarer must have good reason to suspect that the missing queen is offside if he is going to reject the normal finesse. Here is the sort of hand on which the double two-suit squeeze can be useful.

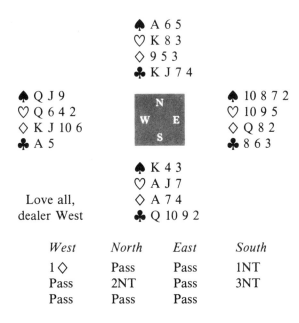

```
                    ♠ A 6 5
                    ♡ K 8 3
                    ◇ 9 5 3
                    ♣ K J 7 4
  ♠ Q J 9                              ♠ 10 8 7 2
  ♡ Q 6 4 2          N                 ♡ 10 9 5
  ◇ K J 10 6     W       E             ◇ Q 8 2
  ♣ A 5              S                 ♣ 8 6 3
                    ♠ K 4 3
                    ♡ A J 7
  Love all,         ◇ A 7 4
  dealer West       ♣ Q 10 9 2
```

West	North	East	South
1 ◇	Pass	Pass	1NT
Pass	2NT	Pass	3NT
Pass	Pass	Pass	

West leads the jack of diamonds and East encourages with the eight. You hold up the ace, but win the next trick when West continues with the six of diamonds to his partner's queen. A club is played to the king and a club returned to the ten and ace. West cashes his remaining diamonds, dummy and East throwing clubs while you part with a spade. West now switches to the queen of spades. How should you play?

You need the rest of the tricks and prospects are not too good. West is marked with the queen of hearts for his opening bid and, since he has only six cards in the minors, there is no possibility of the queen being unguarded. You must hope that East has the ten and nine of hearts, in which case you will be able to squeeze both defenders in the major suits.

To shape up the split menace correctly you must win the spade switch on the table with the ace. The play of the jack of clubs to your queen then leaves the position shown in the diagram.

Your next play of the ten of clubs places the defenders in the familiar, painful dilemma. No matter what they choose as their discards, you are in a position to make the rest of the tricks.

Ambiguity will not be a problem in this case. You have

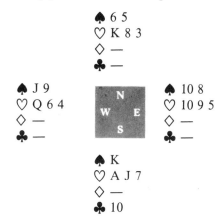

♠ 6 5
♡ K 8 3
◇ —
♣ —

♠ J 9
♡ Q 6 4
◇ —
♣ —

♠ 10 8
♡ 10 9 5
◇ —
♣ —

♠ K
♡ A J 7
◇ —
♣ 10

already seen a heart discard from West, and if he throws another one you can be confident that the queen will drop.

THE DOUBLE VICE

Does the heart position in the above diagram remind you of something you have seen before? East is saddled with the task of keeping a guard to two equals in order to protect a higher card in his partner's hand. The situation bears a marked similarity to the secondary squeeze known as the vice, which we examined in *Strip-Squeezes*.

The double two-suit squeeze is, in fact, the one-loser form of the double vice. The vice is normally a two-loser squeeze, a trick being conceded after the squeeze has taken effect. So it will come as no surprise to you to learn that the double vice also has a two-loser form.

The requirements are a two-card vice menace in the same hand as the squeeze card and a normal two-card menace in the opposite hand, which must also hold two cards in the suit of the vice menace. Here is the basic diagram.

When the ace of clubs is played West cannot afford to bare the ace of hearts, otherwise South will throw the five of spades from the table and duck a heart. So West discards a spade and dummy a heart, and the vice closes around East's heart honours.

When East discards a heart, South crosses to the ace of spades, removing West's exit card, and then plays the heart to establish a trick in the suit.

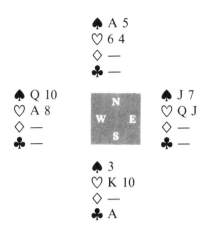

```
              ♠ A 5
              ♡ 6 4
              ◇ —
              ♣ —
♠ Q 10                   ♠ J 7
♡ A 8        N           ♡ Q J
◇ —      W       E       ◇ —
♣ —          S           ♣ —
              ♠ 3
              ♡ K 10
              ◇ —
              ♣ A
```

The vice menace does not have to be K 10 threatening an opponent's Q J. In practice declarer often has something like Q 9 x opposite K x x where one defender has A x x and the other J 10 x.

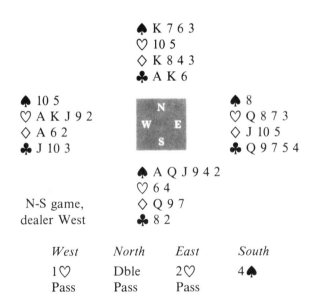

```
                    ♠ K 7 6 3
                    ♡ 10 5
                    ◇ K 8 4 3
                    ♣ A K 6
♠ 10 5                              ♠ 8
♡ A K J 9 2          N              ♡ Q 8 7 3
◇ A 6 2         W        E          ◇ J 10 5
♣ J 10 3             S              ♣ Q 9 7 5 4
                    ♠ A Q J 9 4 2
                    ♡ 6 4
    N-S game,        ◇ Q 9 7
    dealer West      ♣ 8 2
```

West	North	East	South
1♡	Dble	2♡	4♠
Pass	Pass	Pass	

West starts with the ace and king of hearts and continues with the jack of clubs to dummy's ace. How should you plan the play?

Nine tricks are on view but there could be a little difficulty in finding the tenth. West is pretty sure to have the ace of diamonds for his opening bid. It could be guarded only once but it would be unwise to bank on this. The other chance is that East could have the jack and ten of diamonds, in which case it may be possible to squeeze both defenders in the same two suits.

Little is required in the way of preparation. Just run the trumps and hope to reach this position.

The play of the last spade puts West under pressure. He will no doubt discard a club, in which case you throw a diamond from dummy. Now it is East's turn to squirm. Unable to afford the discard of a club, he has to part with a diamond.

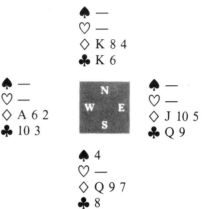

Now it is plain sailing. You play a low diamond, winning with the king if West plays low. After cashing the ace of clubs, you return the diamond to establish your tenth trick in that suit. If West goes up with the ace of diamonds on the first round, you must of course unblock the king to make sure of your tenth trick.

This all looks fairly automatic, but West missed an easy way of defeating the game. We shall take another look at the hand in the chapter on defence.

COPING WITH A BLOCKAGE

Squeezes with irregular entry positions can exist when declarer would have been able to win all the remaining tricks but for a blockage in one of his suits. Here is one of the diagrams from *Simple Squeezes*.

The long menace is in the same hand as the squeeze card, but the fact that dummy's spade is of master rank provides sufficient compensation.

On the play of the ace of clubs West is obliged to unguard one of the majors. If he lets go the heart ace, South plays the ten of spades to dummy's king and scores the heart king. If West parts with a spade South plays the spade

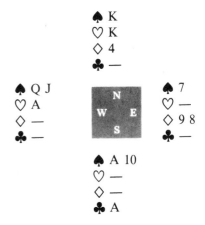

ace next, crashing the missing honour card and promoting his ten. The squeeze just restores to declarer the tricks that are rightfully his.

This arrangement of menaces can function equally well to produce a

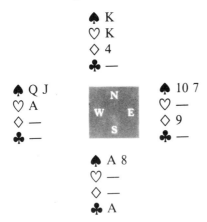

double squeeze. If we change a couple of cards in the South and East hands, we get the position shown in the new diagram.

On the ace of clubs West will no doubt discard a spade. The king of hearts is then thrown from dummy and the pressure switches to East. No matter what East discards, declarer is in a position to take the last two tricks.

The simple squeeze in the top diagram is automatic, working equally well against either opponent, but the double squeeze is positional. Declarer needs to know which defender controls each suit; otherwise he might discard the wrong red menace on the squeeze card.

This point seldom causes any difficulty in practice.

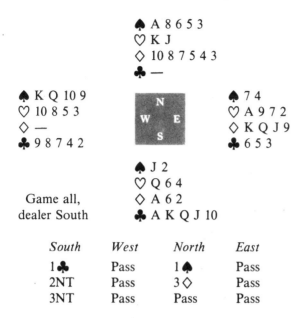

```
              ♠ A 8 6 5 3
              ♡ K J
              ◇ 10 8 7 5 4 3
              ♣ —

♠ K Q 10 9                        ♠ 7 4
♡ 10 8 5 3          N             ♡ A 9 7 2
◇ —            W         E        ◇ K Q J 9
♣ 9 8 7 4 2         S             ♣ 6 5 3

              ♠ J 2
              ♡ Q 6 4
Game all,     ◇ A 6 2
dealer South  ♣ A K Q J 10
```

South	West	North	East
1♣	Pass	1♠	Pass
2NT	Pass	3◇	Pass
3NT	Pass	Pass	Pass

West leads the king of spades against your three no-trumps. You play low from dummy and East contributes the seven. Knowing from the bidding that you will not have more than two cards in the suit, West continues with the queen of spades. This time you take the ace and play the king of hearts from the table. East wins immediately with the ace and switches to the king of diamonds.

In a sense you have nine tricks—one spade, two hearts, one diamond and five clubs—but this lead inconveniently attacks your only entry to hand before you have had a chance to unblock the hearts. Still, you are not too unhappy about the situation at this point. If the diamonds break no worse than 3–1 you will be able to establish an extra diamond trick instead of your second heart. So you play low on the ace of diamonds and receive a jolt when West shows out. East continues with the queen of diamonds and you again play low, but on the next trick your ace of diamonds is knocked out.

The defenders have certainly made life difficult, but the situation is far from hopeless. You have a one-card menace in spades against West, a one-card menace in diamonds against East and a master heart in dummy to serve as an entry. On the play of the clubs neither defender will be able to keep two hearts. Just run your long suit to reach the diagram position.

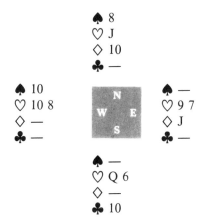

When the ten of clubs is played West has to part with a heart in order to keep his spade winner. The eight of spades is discarded from dummy and it is East's turn to feel the pressure. If East also discards a heart, you simply cash the queen of hearts and score your ninth trick with the heart six.

This was not a difficult hand to play, but there were a couple of points worth noting. First, you had to tackle the hearts by playing the king rather than the jack. If the highest heart had been left in dummy you would have been defeated, for there is no such thing as a double jettison squeeze.

The second point is that it was not strictly necessary to rectify the count by ducking twice in diamonds. The squeeze would have worked just as well with two or even three losers. It could then have been termed a double stepping-stone.

THE DOUBLE STEPPING-STONE

This is the two-loser version of the squeeze we have just been looking at.

A blocked suit is still the main feature, but the basic diagram is a four-card rather than a three-card ending.

South needs three out of the last four tricks and he would have no trouble but for the blocked position in diamonds. The squeeze is a rescue manoeuvre which allows him to overcome the blockage.

Both defenders have what appears to be an idle card. On the play of the ace of clubs it is natural for West to throw the four of spades and East the two of hearts. In fact they have been

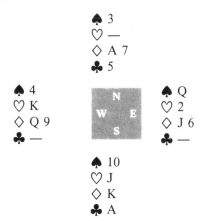

squeezed out of their exit cards. South then unblocks the king of diamonds and continues with either his spade or his heart, using a defender's hand as a stepping-stone to reach the ace of diamonds.

If one defender discards a diamond on the club ace, South again unblocks in diamonds and exits towards the other defender. And if both defenders throw diamonds, South overtakes the king of diamonds with the ace and scores the diamond seven. Accurate card-reading is essential in these situations.

The fact that dummy holds an idle card makes the squeeze fully automatic. It would work just as well with the East and West hands interchanged, and the squeeze-card may lie in either hand. But note that the top card in the blocked suit must not be on its own, otherwise you would lose the overtaking option.

You might get through a lifetime without encountering a double stepping-stone, but you could be lucky enough to recognise such a situation and bring the squeeze to a successful conclusion. A hand I used in *Advanced Play at Bridge* is worth another look.

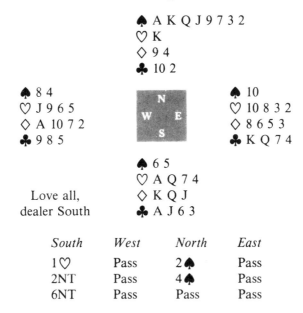

♠ A K Q J 9 7 3 2
♡ K
◇ 9 4
♣ 10 2

♠ 8 4
♡ J 9 6 5
◇ A 10 7 2
♣ 9 8 5

♠ 10
♡ 10 8 3 2
◇ 8 6 5 3
♣ K Q 7 4

♠ 6 5
♡ A Q 7 4
◇ K Q J
♣ A J 6 3

Love all,
dealer South

South	West	North	East
1♡	Pass	2♠	Pass
2NT	Pass	4♠	Pass
6NT	Pass	Pass	Pass

West leads the nine of clubs and East puts in the queen. How do you plan the play?

At the time it seemed a good idea to have the lead coming up to your hand, but you note disconsolately that six spades would have been easy. This unfriendly club lead attacks your outside entry before you have had a chance to unblock the hearts or drive out the ace of diamonds. Your twelve tricks have suddenly been reduced to eleven. What can you do about it?

You might think of ducking the first trick in the hope that East will not find the diamond switch, but this is really fuzzy thinking. If East has the ace of diamonds he is sure to cash it, and if West has the ace the slam is unbeatable.

Win the first trick and hit the defenders with an avalanche of spades.

Here is the ending you are aiming for.

When the last spade is played, neither defender will be able to keep three hearts, his own minor-suit winner *and* a card in partner's suit. If you keep count of the hearts and watch the discards carefully you should have every chance of getting it right.

If both defenders choose to abandon hearts, you can simply overtake dummy's king of hearts with your ace. Otherwise

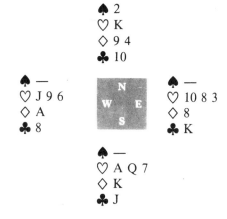

you will play the heart seven on dummy's king and exit towards whichever opponent you think has two hearts left at this stage.

THE DOUBLE WINKLE

This is another way of overcoming a blockage. Both defenders are squeezed in the same two suits, and have the choice of allowing a

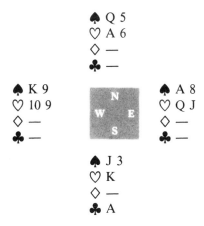

stepping-stone ending or unblocking their high cards. In the latter event declarer winkles a trick for a card which is no higher than third in rank. Here is the basic diagram.

South leads the ace of clubs and discards the small spade from dummy, and the defenders are under heavy pressure. If they both discard hearts, South overtakes the king of hearts and scores the six of hearts. If one defender discards a low spade, South unblocks the king of hearts and exits with a spade for the stepping-stone ending. And if someone discards a high spade, South can exit in spades with or without unblocking in hearts. He is assured of a third trick in either spades or hearts.

The double winkle will sometimes help you to bring home an 'impossible' contract. Here is an example.

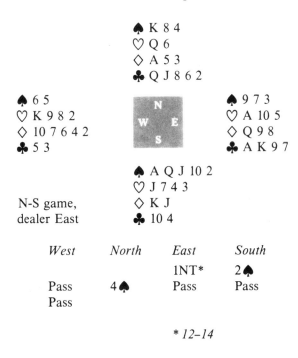

```
                    ♠ K 8 4
                    ♡ Q 6
                    ◇ A 5 3
                    ♣ Q J 8 6 2
    ♠ 6 5                          ♠ 9 7 3
    ♡ K 9 8 2                      ♡ A 10 5
    ◇ 10 7 6 4 2                   ◇ Q 9 8
    ♣ 5 3                          ♣ A K 9 7
                    ♠ A Q J 10 2
                    ♡ J 7 4 3
    N-S game,       ◇ K J
    dealer East     ♣ 10 4
```

West	North	East	South
		1NT*	2♠
Pass	4♠	Pass	Pass
Pass			

12-14

West leads the five of clubs and East plays three rounds of the suit, forcing you to ruff with the ten for safety. West discards the two of diamonds, and both defenders follow when you cash the ace of spades. What now?

You were lucky to escape a heart switch, and you may now have a chance if East has the queen of diamonds. But there is a terrible communication problem. How can you take the diamond finesse and later return to dummy to enjoy the third diamond?

[70]

You might think of trying a finesse of the spade eight on the second round, but this is both risky and unnecessary. If East has the diamond queen and the trumps are 3–2, the game is yours for the taking.

Both the bidding and the play indicate that the heart honours will be divided, in which case a double winkle should deliver the contract. Play the queen of spades and continue with a spade to the king. Two of your hearts go away on the long clubs, and then you play a low diamond for a finesse of the jack. This position has been reached.

You have an automatic discard of the six of hearts from dummy when you play the last trump, but the defenders have no cards to spare. If both discard diamonds, you have an

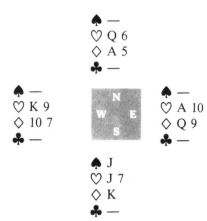

```
                ♠ —
                ♡ Q 6
                ◇ A 5
                ♣ —
♠ —                          ♠ —
♡ K 9                        ♡ A 10
◇ 10 7                       ◇ Q 9
♣ —                          ♣ —
                ♠ J
                ♡ J 7
                ◇ K
                ♣ —
```

overtaking situation. If one discards a low heart you have a stepping-stone ending. And if either unblocks his heart honour you are in a position to winkle a trick for your jack of hearts.

5

Double Squeeze Defence

Once you become familiar with the arrangements of entries and menaces that can result in a double squeeze, you can look forward to a rich harvest of extra tricks. Naturally, you will wish to deny declarer those extra tricks when you are defending. In the earlier chapters we have already noted some points of interest for the defence. Now it is time to introduce some order into the subject by examining the defensive options in a methodical way.

The defenders are fortunate in one respect, for as squeezes become more complex they also become more vulnerable to attack. The more machinery declarer has to deploy, the more chances the defenders have of throwing a spanner into the works. This does not mean that double squeeze defence is easy. The main problem in defending against any squeeze is one of recognition. You have to spot the danger in advance and take prompt action, for if a successful defence is possible it will normally have to be launched at an early stage in the play. A pre-emptive strike is often the only way of preventing a squeeze from maturing. Once you are in the grip of a fully-established squeeze there may be little you can do.

The defenders have to direct their main efforts, as usual, against the three features that are essential for the execution of any squeeze—entries, menaces and timing. Since the attack on entries is the most fruitful source of profit we shall start with this.

THE ATTACK ON ENTRIES

No squeeze can function without certain minimum entry requirements.

In the case of the double squeeze the most vital entry for declarer is in the suit of the double menace—the suit in which both defenders are threatened. In many cases, therefore, this is the proper target for attack. Consider this hand.

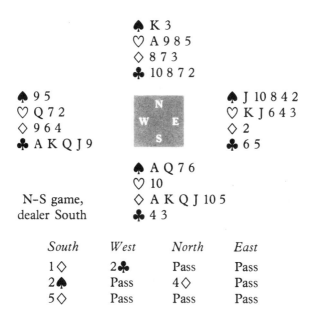

♠ K 3
♡ A 9 8 5
◇ 8 7 3
♣ 10 8 7 2

♠ 9 5
♡ Q 7 2
◇ 9 6 4
♣ A K Q J 9

♠ J 10 8 4 2
♡ K J 6 4 3
◇ 2
♣ 6 5

♠ A Q 7 6
♡ 10
◇ A K Q J 10 5
♣ 4 3

N–S game,
dealer South

South	West	North	East
1◇	2♣	Pass	Pass
2♠	Pass	4◇	Pass
5◇	Pass	Pass	Pass

West starts with the ace and king of clubs and is gratified to win the first two tricks. How should he continue?

Most defenders would be disinclined to strain the brain on this hand. After all, West has what looks like a perfectly safe club continuation. But let us examine in detail what is likely to happen if West plays a third round of clubs.

Declarer will ruff the third club and test the diamonds with the ace and king. When East shows out on the second round South will reject any idea of trying to ruff a spade in dummy. East is likely to have the spade length, in which case a double squeeze will make a certainty of the hand.

South will draw the outstanding trump, play off three rounds of spades, and continue with trumps to reach the position shown in the diagram.

On the play of the last diamond West has to discard a heart in order to keep his club winner. The ten of clubs is thrown from the table and East finds the pressure too much for him.

The outcome would have been different if West had been more alert at trick three. It was not too hard to foresee the looming danger of the double squeeze. The club menace was

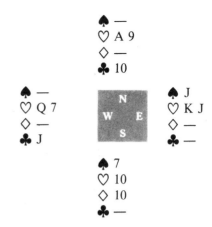

♠ —
♡ A 9
◇ —
♣ 10

♠ —
♡ Q 7
◇ —
♣ J

♠ J
♡ K J
◇ —
♣ —

♠ 7
♡ 10
◇ 10
♣ —

visible in dummy, as was the potential double menace in hearts, and it required no great effort of imagination to visualise the spade threat against East.

A defender familiar with double squeezes might have found the proper medicine of a switch to a low heart at trick three. This takes out the entry to the double menace and removes all real chance of a squeeze. Declarer would then have been left with little option but to try to ruff a spade on the table, and West would have scored a trump as the setting trick.

On that hand a single thrust was enough to take out the entry for the double squeeze. Sometimes a sustained attack on the double menace is required.

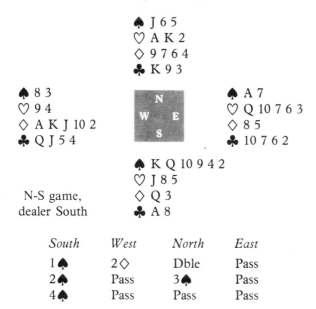

```
              ♠ J 6 5
              ♡ A K 2
              ◇ 9 7 6 4
              ♣ K 9 3
♠ 8 3                           ♠ A 7
♡ 9 4                           ♡ Q 10 7 6 3
◇ A K J 10 2                    ◇ 8 5
♣ Q J 5 4                       ♣ 10 7 6 2
              ♠ K Q 10 9 4 2
              ♡ J 8 5
N-S game,      ◇ Q 3
dealer South   ♣ A 8
```

South	West	North	East
1♠	2◇	Dble	Pass
2♠	Pass	3♠	Pass
4♠	Pass	Pass	Pass

West starts with the ace and king of diamonds. How should he continue?

Declarer is likely to have six spades, and West must hope that his partner can produce a trick in one of the black suits. If East has the ace of clubs the contract is sure to be defeated, but East could have the ace of spades instead. In that case declarer will have nine tricks—five spades, two hearts and two clubs—and the threats are in place for a positional double squeeze. There is a diamond menace against West, a heart menace against East and a double menace in clubs. Unless West takes the right counter-measures the ending will be as shown in the diagram.

When the last spade is played neither defender can hold two clubs and the game rolls home.

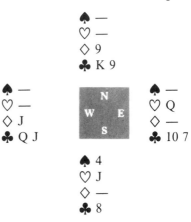

```
              ♠ —
              ♡ —
              ◇ 9
              ♣ K 9
♠ —                     ♠ —
♡ —                     ♡ Q
◇ J                     ◇ —
♣ Q J                   ♣ 10 7
              ♠ 4
              ♡ J
              ◇ —
              ♣ 8
```

The right move for West is to lead the queen of clubs at trick three. If East has the ace of clubs this will gather in two quick tricks in the suit. As it happens, the queen of clubs launches an attack on declarer's double menace. South wins with the ace and tackles the trumps, but East takes his ace and continues with a club, killing the double menace and destroying all chance of a squeeze.

Note that there is no real risk for West in switching to the queen of clubs. If declarer has the ten of clubs as well as the ace, he is destined to make the game anyway.

Often, when working out the best defence to a double squeeze you have to consider the dangers of a simple squeeze as well. Here is an example.

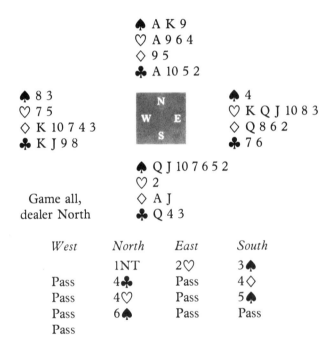

```
                    ♠ A K 9
                    ♡ A 9 6 4
                    ◇ 9 5
                    ♣ A 10 5 2
   ♠ 8 3                              ♠ 4
   ♡ 7 5                              ♡ K Q J 10 8 3
   ◇ K 10 7 4 3         N            ◇ Q 8 6 2
   ♣ K J 9 8         W     E         ♣ 7 6
                        S
                    ♠ Q J 10 7 6 5 2
                    ♡ 2
  Game all,         ◇ A J
  dealer North      ♣ Q 4 3
```

West	North	East	South
	1NT	2♡	3♠
Pass	4♣	Pass	4◇
Pass	4♡	Pass	5♠
Pass	6♠	Pass	Pass
Pass			

Your lead of the seven of hearts goes to dummy's ace and East follows with the king. Declarer draws trumps with the ace and king, East discarding the three of hearts on the second round. A small club is played from dummy to the seven, queen and king. How should you continue?

There can be no heart trick for the defence. Declarer can be counted for seven spades, one heart and three clubs to judge from partner's play of the seven. He will therefore have two diamonds. With the help of the two red aces and the club finesse, declarer has eleven tricks, and the danger is that the twelfth may come from a squeeze. If South's diamonds are as good as A Q you can do nothing but wait for the inevitable minor-suit squeeze.

Even if partner has the queen of diamonds the position is full of danger. Declarer may now be able to produce a double squeeze using diamonds as the double menace. It is the inverted positional type where the double menace is in the same hand as the squeeze card, but you can see that it will work because the entry to dummy is in your suit. Suppose you return the nine of clubs at this point. Declarer will finesse the ten, ruff a heart and run the rest of the trumps. This will be the end position.

The play of the last trump will squeeze you out of your diamond guard. The club five will be discarded from dummy, and then the play of a club to the ace will squeeze partner in the red suits.

Once again, the way to break up the double squeeze is to attack the double menace. But in this case, with declarer hold-ing the diamond jack, it is not good enough to lead a small

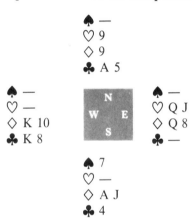

diamond at trick five. Partner's queen will be gobbled up by the ace, and you will be subject to a simple squeeze in the minor suits on the run of the spades. To kill all squeeze chances you must lead the king of diamonds. East can never be squeezed in the red suits once the diamond entry has gone.

The slam would have been defeated more easily, of course, if you had led a diamond originally. This game would be much simpler if we could always play in double-dummy fashion.

FRUSTRATING A VIENNA COUP

On certain hands the only way of defeating a double squeeze is to find the killing lead at trick one. Sometimes you will be lucky enough to receive a second chance, but you may have to tread a narrow path to achieve success. Consider this hand.

                  ♠ A K 7
                  ♡ Q J 4
                  ◇ 10 7 3
                  ♣ A K 8 5

    ♠ J 9 3   ♠ Q 10 6 5 2
    ♡ A 6 3   ♡ 2
    ◇ Q J 9 5   ◇ 8 6 4 2
    ♣ 9 4 3   ♣ Q 10 6

                  ♠ 8 4
                  ♡ K 10 9 8 7 5
    Love all,   ◇ A K
    dealer South ♣ J 7 2

South	West	North	East
1♡	Pass	2NT	Pass
3♡	Pass	3♠	Pass
4♡	Pass	5♣	Pass
5◇	Pass	6♡	Pass
Pass	Pass		

Forceful bidding by North propels his partner into a borderline slam, and you select the queen of diamonds as your opening lead. East contributes the four and South wins with the ace. A low heart is played to dummy's jack, East following with the two. Next comes the queen of hearts on which East discards the two of diamonds. How do you plan the defence?

Declarer must surely have the king of diamonds, which gives him eleven tricks. Partner will need to have both black queens if the defence is to have a chance. Even so, the threat of a double squeeze looms ahead. Dummy holds a single menace in diamonds plus a double menace in spades, and it is highly likely that declarer has a club menace against partner in his own hand.

The double menace in spades is accompanied by an extra winner and is therefore immune to attack at this stage. You may consider winning the second trump and returning a diamond to take out declarer's bare king, but a sorry fate is in store for you if you do. Winning the king of diamonds, declarer will unblock the top clubs and then run the trumps to reach this position:

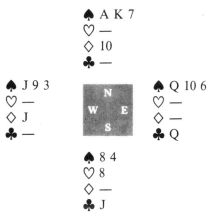

♠ A K 7
♡ —
◇ 10
♣ —

♠ J 9 3
♡ —
◇ J
♣ —

♠ Q 10 6
♡ —
◇ —
♣ Q

♠ 8 4
♡ 8
◇ —
♣ J

When the last trump is played, you have to keep your master diamond and partner his master club and neither of you is able to hold three spades.

The timing of the strike is all-important in squeeze defence. To defeat this squeeze all you had to do was hold up the ace of hearts until the third round and *then* play a second diamond. This has the effect of preventing declarer from executing his Vienna Coup in clubs. If South unblocks the clubs he has no way of returning to hand without destroying one of his vital menaces. And with the clubs blocked the squeeze cannot work.

No doubt you have seen the alternative way of beating the slam. If West leads a spade initially and continues with a second spade when in with the ace of hearts, the double menace is destroyed and no squeeze is possible.

AUTO-DEFENCE

We have seen that an attack on the double menace is often the right course for the defenders. This is especially true when the squeeze is of the inverted automatic type. Such squeezes are highly flexible and relatively easy to play, for the three-card double menace creates space for an idle card in the opposite hand. An attack on the double menace converts the squeeze to the more rigid positional form. It may well kill the squeeze completely, and it will at least make declarer's task much more difficult. Take the East seat on this next hand.

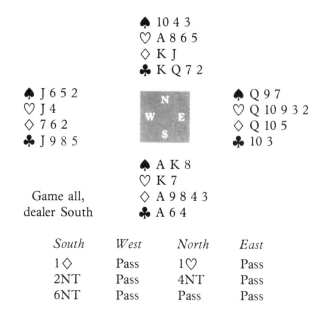

```
                      ♠ 10 4 3
                      ♡ A 8 6 5
                      ◇ K J
                      ♣ K Q 7 2
   ♠ J 6 5 2                             ♠ Q 9 7
   ♡ J 4              N                  ♡ Q 10 9 3 2
   ◇ 7 6 2        W       E              ◇ Q 10 5
   ♣ J 9 8 5          S                  ♣ 10 3
                      ♠ A K 8
                      ♡ K 7
   Game all,         ◇ A 9 8 4 3
   dealer South      ♣ A 6 4
```

South	West	North	East
1◇	Pass	1♡	Pass
2NT	Pass	4NT	Pass
6NT	Pass	Pass	Pass

West leads the jack of hearts against the slam. South wins in hand with the king and plays the three of diamonds to the two, jack and queen. How do you continue?

To judge from partner's play of the two of diamonds, declarer has five cards in the suit. South is also marked with all the missing aces and kings. Partner will need to have a pair of black jacks to give the defence a chance.

Partner may well have a club stopper, but declarer has eleven top tricks and all the machinery he needs to operate a double squeeze with spades as the long menace. It is the inverted automatic type which will present few problems.

If you continue with a heart to the ace at this point for instance, declarer will have an easy time. After unblocking the king of diamonds he will cash the club king, play a club to his ace and then run the rest of the diamonds to reach this position:

Dummy has an idle card—a spade—to throw on the last diamond, but West is forced to part with a spade in order to keep his guard in clubs. The play of a club to the queen then ruins East in a similar manner.

The outcome may be different if you switch to the seven of spades when in with the queen of diamonds. This attack on the double menace converts the automatic squeeze into a

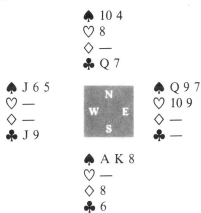

positional one, and declarer can now get home only if he plays his cards in precisely the right order. The inverted double positional squeeze requires that all winners in the suit menacing the right-hand opponent be played off before the squeeze card (the last diamond). If, after winning the spade switch, declarer plays a heart to the ace, unblocks the king of diamonds and plays two rounds of clubs, ending in hand, he can reach this position:

Once again the play of the last diamond squeezes West, but there is no idle card to throw from dummy and the position is full of ambiguity for South. He may well go wrong at this point by discarding the heart and banking on an even division of the clubs.

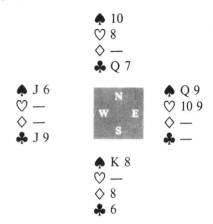

Declarer might also have gone astray at an earlier stage by playing off three rounds of clubs and keeping the ace of hearts on the table. Once the club entry to dummy has gone there is no double squeeze.

THE ATTACK ON MENACES

When there is no possibility of launching an effective attack on entries, the defenders have to look for other ways of protecting themselves against a double squeeze. A good alternative is to wipe out one of declarer's menaces. When any sort of squeeze situation is building up, killing a menace is usually a complete answer.

Here is a simple hand.

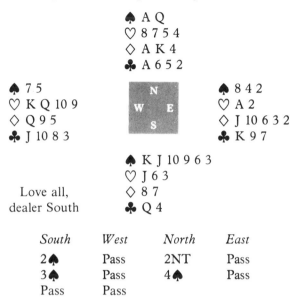

```
              ♠ A Q
              ♡ 8 7 5 4
              ◇ A K 4
              ♣ A 6 5 2
♠ 7 5                              ♠ 8 4 2
♡ K Q 10 9        N               ♡ A 2
◇ Q 9 5        W     E            ◇ J 10 6 3 2
♣ J 10 8 3        S               ♣ K 9 7
              ♠ K J 10 9 6 3
              ♡ J 6 3
Love all,     ◇ 8 7
dealer South  ♣ Q 4
```

South	West	North	East
2♠	Pass	2NT	Pass
3♠	Pass	4♠	Pass
Pass	Pass		

South opens with a weak two bid and eventually lands in the hazardous contract of four spades. Looking at all four hands, one can easily see that three no-trumps would have been a happier spot.

Against four spades you select the natural lead of the king of hearts. Partner overtakes with the ace and returns the two of hearts to the jack and queen. When you continue with the ten of hearts East discards the two of diamonds. What now?

Declarer is likely to have six solid spade tricks and you can see three outside winners on the table. Partner will need to have the king of clubs to give the defence a chance, but if declarer has the queen of clubs you may be in some danger from a double squeeze.

There is no need to attack entries on this occasion and no need to think too hard. Just follow your instincts. Most defenders will feel a natural urge to continue with the fourth heart, and sometimes the natural move is the right one. The play of the nine of hearts squashes the heart menace in dummy and destroys all chance of a squeeze. On the run of the spades West can keep diamonds and East clubs, and declarer has nowhere to go for his tenth trick.

Be sure to appreciate what would have happened if you had tried something fancy like attacking the entry in the suit of the double menace at trick four. Winning the diamond switch with the king, declarer would have unblocked the ace of clubs and then played out his trumps to reach the position shown in the diagram.

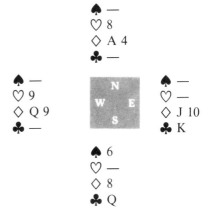

♠ —
♡ 8
◇ A 4
♣ —

♠ —   ♠ —
♡ 9   ♡ —
◇ Q 9   ◇ J 10
♣ —   ♣ K

♠ 6
♡ —
◇ 8
♣ Q

On the play of the last spade you have to keep your heart nine and throw a diamond. The heart is discarded from the table and East is squeezed in the minor suits. You are left with the agonised reflection that by leaving the eight of hearts in dummy you have scored an 'own goal.'

SHARING THE LOAD

When no direct attack on a menace is possible, the defenders can often avert danger by sharing the burden of guarding the menaces in a sensible manner. In many positions declarer has no genuine squeeze provided that the defenders exercise normal care: all he can produce is a pseudo-squeeze. Unfortunately a pseudo-squeeze can feel very much like the real thing from the defenders' side of the table, and one careless discard may be enough to transform it into a genuine squeeze.

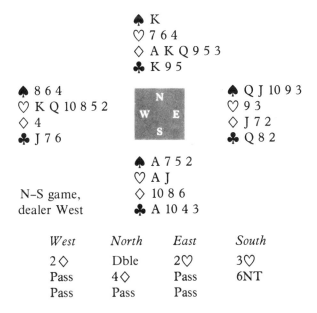

♠ K
♡ 7 6 4
◇ A K Q 9 5 3
♣ K 9 5

♠ 8 6 4
♡ K Q 10 8 5 2
◇ 4
♣ J 7 6

♠ Q J 10 9 3
♡ 9 3
◇ J 7 2
♣ Q 8 2

♠ A 7 5 2
♡ A J
◇ 10 8 6
♣ A 10 4 3

N–S game,
dealer West

West	North	East	South
2◇	Dble	2♡	3♡
Pass	4◇	Pass	6NT
Pass	Pass	Pass	

You open a multi-coloured two diamonds showing, in this instance, a weak two in hearts. This does not intimidate your opponents, who take only two rounds of bidding to reach the small slam in no-trumps.

On your lead of the king of hearts East plays the nine and declarer the jack. No switch looks attractive, so you continue with hearts, declarer winning with the ace as partner follows with the three. South now makes a nuisance of himself by running the diamonds. Your first three discards are easy enough since you can spare three hearts. Meanwhile East throws the queen of spades on the fourth diamond and South the two of spades. On the fifth diamond East discards the nine of spades and South the three of clubs. What is your discard?

You cannot afford to throw your last heart and it seems natural to part with a 'worthless' spade. But those spades are not really without value. If you discard one you will turn the pseudo-squeeze into a genuine double squeeze.

West will be forced to discard a club on the sixth diamond, and after unblocking the king of spades South will enter his hand with the ace of clubs to reach this position:

The play of the ace of spades squeezes you in clubs and hearts and the slam is made.

There was no excuse for your careless discard of a spade. By throwing the queen and then the nine of spades partner had supplied you with the right information. It was clear that declarer's second spade could be no higher than the seven. Your eight was therefore bound to be a sufficient guard in the

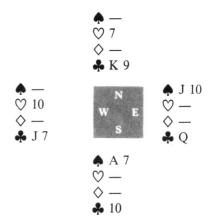

suit. It was your duty to look after the two disconnected menaces in the major suits, leaving partner to guard the clubs. If you had discarded a club on the fifth diamond, partner could have thrown another spade on the sixth round. By following declarer's discard on this trick, you could then have made sure of defeating the slam.

THE ATTACK ON TIMING

Another sure way of defeating a squeeze is by denying declarer the correct timing. Most double squeezes operate only at the direct level, which means that declarer must be in a position to win all the tricks but one at the time when the squeeze card is led. If he has two losers and is unable to rectify the count, the squeeze must fail.

Defenders have to guard against tightening up the position for declarer by cashing a trick too many at an early stage. Danger may lurk in the simplest of contracts. Here, for example, is an ordinary three no-trumps.

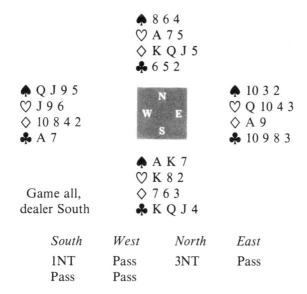

```
                    ♠ 8 6 4
                    ♡ A 7 5
                    ◇ K Q J 5
                    ♣ 6 5 2
♠ Q J 9 5                           ♠ 10 3 2
♡ J 9 6                             ♡ Q 10 4 3
◇ 10 8 4 2                          ◇ A 9
♣ A 7                              ♣ 10 9 8 3
                    ♠ A K 7
                    ♡ K 8 2
Game all,            ◇ 7 6 3
dealer South         ♣ K Q J 4
```

South	West	North	East
1NT	Pass	3NT	Pass
Pass	Pass		

South opens a strong no-trump and North raises to game. West leads the queen of spades which is allowed to hold the first trick. Declarer wins the next spade and plays a diamond to the king. East takes his ace and knocks out the remaining spade stopper. Declarer plays a second diamond to dummy's queen and returns a club to the queen and ace. This is the position:

West has worked hard to establish the thirteenth spade. It seems natural to cash it at this point, and that is what nine out of ten players would do. But there is an unhappy sequel for the defenders. A club is discarded from dummy on the fourth spade while East and South throw hearts. Suddenly

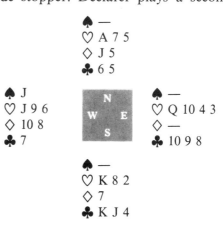

```
                ♠ —
                ♡ A 7 5
                ◇ J 5
                ♣ 6 5
♠ J                          ♠ —
♡ J 9 6                      ♡ Q 10 4 3
◇ 10 8                       ◇ —
♣ 7                         ♣ 10 9 8
                ♠ —
                ♡ K 8 2
                ◇ 7
                ♣ K J 4
```

declarer is in a position to win all but one of the remaining tricks and the timing is right for a double squeeze. It does not matter which card West plays next. Each defender is squeezed by the play of the master cards in his partner's suit and the game is made.

A good rule in such situations is not to cash a fourth defensive trick unless you can see where the setting trick is coming from. If West leads any card except the jack of spades in the diagram position, the declarer must lose two tricks.

Constant vigilance is required in squeeze or pseudo-squeeze situations. There may be no chance to recover from an early slip.

```
                    ♠ Q 5
                    ♡ A J 10 8 3
                    ◇ A Q 6 4
                    ♣ Q 7
  ♠ 6 2                            ♠ A 10 9 7 3
  ♡ K 9 6 5            N           ♡ Q 7 2
  ◇ J 10 9 7      W        E       ◇ 5 3
  ♣ 9 8 4              S           ♣ 10 6 3
                    ♠ K J 8 4
                    ♡ 4
  Game all,         ◇ K 8 2
  dealer South      ♣ A K J 5 2
```

South	West	North	East
1♣	Pass	1♡	Pass
1♠	Pass	2◇	Pass
3NT	Pass	6NT	Pass
Pass	Pass		

A heart lead would be devastating but, not being gifted with second sight, West leads the jack of diamonds. South wins in hand with the king and plays the four of spades to the queen and ace. How should East continue?

If South has five running clubs, as seems likely, he can be counted for eleven top tricks. The danger is that the twelfth may come from a double squeeze. What can East do about it?

At this stage, regrettably, nothing. The chance to beat the slam has come and gone. If East returns a spade, a diamond or a club, declarer will play off his winners in spades and diamonds and then run the clubs to reach the diagram position.

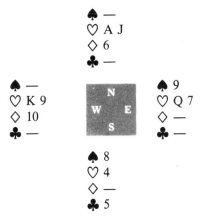

On the play of the last club West has to throw a heart in order to keep his diamond winner. The diamond is discarded from the table and East finds the pressure too great.

East might launch an attack on the double menace by returning a heart at trick three, but this does not save the day. If East plays a low heart to the king and ace, he will later be squeezed in the majors. And if he plays the queen of hearts to knock out the ace, West will be subject to a red-suit squeeze.

East should have done his thinking a trick earlier. Then he might have found the winning defence of allowing the queen of spades to hold the second trick. He has to duck the second spade as well, playing the nine to force an honour from declarer. Now South has eleven tricks, but since he has failed to rectify his loser count he has no chance of making a twelfth trick. It's all in the timing.

One further example shows the need for defenders to remain alert at all times.

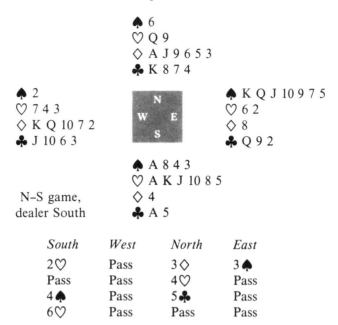

	♠ 6	
	♡ Q 9	
	◇ A J 9 6 5 3	
	♣ K 8 7 4	

♠ 2		♠ K Q J 10 9 7 5
♡ 7 4 3		♡ 6 2
◇ K Q 10 7 2		◇ 8
♣ J 10 6 3		♣ Q 9 2

	♠ A 8 4 3	
N–S game,	♡ A K J 10 8 5	
dealer South	◇ 4	
	♣ A 5	

South	West	North	East
2♡	Pass	3◇	3♠
Pass	Pass	4♡	Pass
4♠	Pass	5♣	Pass
6♡	Pass	Pass	Pass

South began with an Acol two bid and eventually reached the reasonable contract of six hearts. West found the best lead of a trump and the trick was won in dummy. Declarer cashed the ace of diamonds and continued with a small diamond on which East discarded the king of spades. South ruffed in hand, cashed the ace of spades and ruffed a small spade with the heart queen. Another diamond was played and when East discarded a spade South did likewise, giving West an unexpected trick. West did his best by returning a club, but declarer won with the ace and ran his trumps to reach the diagram position.

The play of the ten of hearts put the defenders through the mangle in the familiar way, and

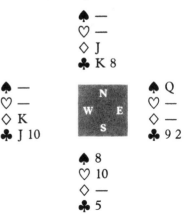

	♠ —	
	♡ —	
	◇ J	
	♣ K 8	

♠ —		♠ Q
♡ —		♡ —
◇ K		◇ —
♣ J 10		♣ 9 2

	♠ 8	
	♡ 10	
	◇ —	
	♣ 5	

dummy's eight of clubs scored the twelfth trick for declarer.

What could the defenders have done about this and who was at fault? East stands condemned as the guilty party. It was clear from an early stage that declarer had only eleven tricks and would need a squeeze to bring home his slam. When the third diamond was played from the table, East might have foreseen that declarer intended to pass this trick to West in order to rectify his loser count.

To prevent this, all East had to do was to toss his second trump on the table. It is a small trump but it throws a giant spanner into the works, for declarer dare not duck a trick to East who has spades ready to cash. South has to over-ruff on the third round of diamonds and he has no further chance to rectify the count. The timing is all wrong for declarer and the squeeze simply fizzles out.

DEFENDING A TWO-LOSER SQUEEZE

The two-loser double squeezes are those such as the double vice whereby both defenders are squeezed in the same two suits. Declarer knocks out the enemy stopper in the suit of the special menace *after* the squeeze has taken effect. Sometimes there is nothing the defenders can do about it, but on certain hands there is no need to allow such a position to arise. It is always a complete answer if the defender who anticipates gaining the lead in the ending can keep an outside winner.

Let us take another look at a hand from Chapter 4.

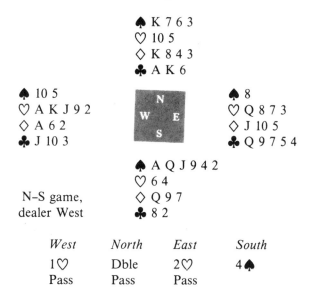

```
                    ♠ K 7 6 3
                    ♡ 10 5
                    ◇ K 8 4 3
                    ♣ A K 6
    ♠ 10 5                          ♠ 8
    ♡ A K J 9 2                     ♡ Q 8 7 3
    ◇ A 6 2                         ◇ J 10 5
    ♣ J 10 3                        ♣ Q 9 7 5 4
                    ♠ A Q J 9 4 2
                    ♡ 6 4
N–S game,           ◇ Q 9 7
dealer West         ♣ 8 2
```

West	North	East	South
West	*North*	*East*	*South*
1♡	Dble	2♡	4♠
Pass	Pass	Pass	

West cashed two top hearts and switched to the jack of clubs, which was won by dummy's ace. With nothing to try except a two-suit double squeeze, South let loose an avalanche of trumps. This was the position after four rounds:

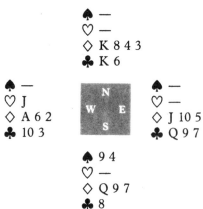

When the nine of spades was played, West let go the jack of hearts in order to keep guards in both minors. This was a serious error. South was known to have another trump left and West was bound to be squeezed out of his club guard at the next trick. The right defence is to let the club go early and keep the winning heart.

What can South do? If he plays off the last trump, West can discard either a club or a diamond and East can happily part with a diamond. When West comes in with the ace of diamonds he cashes the jack of hearts to put the contract one down.

THE AMBIGUITY FACTOR

Many of the squeeze positions that we have studied contain an uncomfortable element of ambiguity. Declarer can succeed if his card-reading is accurate, but there is no need to make it easy for him. Defenders must learn, as a last resort, how to turn the ambiguity factor to their advantage. By discarding in a deceptive manner they may be able to point declarer in the wrong direction.

Here is a typical double ruffing squeeze.

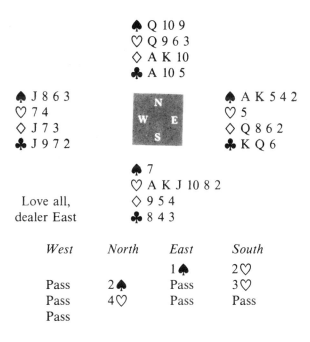

	♠ Q 10 9	
	♡ Q 9 6 3	
	◇ A K 10	
	♣ A 10 5	
♠ J 8 6 3		♠ A K 5 4 2
♡ 7 4		♡ 5
◇ J 7 3		◇ Q 8 6 2
♣ J 9 7 2		♣ K Q 6
	♠ 7	
	♡ A K J 10 8 2	
Love all,	◇ 9 5 4	
dealer East	♣ 8 4 3	

West	North	East	South
		1 ♠	2 ♡
Pass	2 ♠	Pass	3 ♡
Pass	4 ♡	Pass	Pass
Pass			

Rejecting the simple no-trump game, North places the contract in four hearts. West leads the three of spades to his partner's king. East switches to the king of clubs and declarer holds up the ace until the third round.

Needing the rest of the tricks, South has to choose between risking a double diamond finesse and trying for a double ruffing squeeze. Wisely he adopts the latter course and runs the trumps.

South is marked with nine tricks and the ending is foreseeable. There is little hope for the defenders if they follow the course of least resistance, each keeping two spades and three diamonds. This is an occasion for a spot of deceptive discarding, but close co-operation is needed to make it effective.

Suppose that, on the first four trumps, East discards his three small spades and West lets go a club and a diamond. This will be the position:

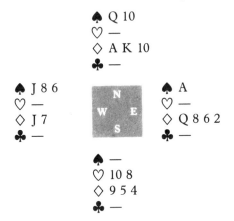

Declarer knows that West began with the jack of spades and East with the ace. But he cannot be sure whether East started with five or six spades. On the next trump West can give South a further nudge in the wrong direction by throwing the eight of spades. Dummy discards a diamond and so does East.

Now, after a diamond to the king, it is quite likely that declarer will do the wrong thing by playing the queen of spades, hoping to pin the jack. His confidence in his card-reading will receive a shattering blow when he has to lose a spade trick at the end.

The defenders have nothing to lose by resorting to deception in such situations. It's better than submitting to sure defeat.

6

Exercises

This is your chance to flex your mental muscles. The exercises are
designed to test your ability over a wide range of double squeeze
situations. Only two hands are shown to begin with in order to
reproduce as far as possible the conditions of play at the bridge table.
Working through a varied body of problems in a theoretical setting,
where success or failure does not really matter, should give you the
confidence needed to tackle similar problems when they arise in your
regular games.

The road to rapid improvement lies in making a real effort to solve
each problem for yourself before going on to read the solution. Do not
be too rigid in your thinking. You should consider a double squeeze on
every hand but be prepared to reject the squeeze if you spot a more
likely line of play. You will find nothing in the exercises that has not been
covered in the earlier chapters, so your performance in the test will fairly
reflect the knowledge you have absorbed from a first reading of the
book. Take five points for each correct answer, and your score over the
twenty problems will give you a percentage figure. Anything over 60% is
a reasonable score for someone new to double squeeze play. Those who
do less well should read the book once more and try the test again in a
few months.

Exercise 1

♠ K 6 4
♡ K Q 6 5
◇ A J 10 4
♣ J 9

Love all, dealer South

South	West	North	East
1♣	Pass	1◇	Pass
2NT	Pass	4NT	Pass
6NT	Pass	Pass	Pass

♠ A 7
♡ A 7 2
◇ 6 5 2
♣ A K Q 10 5

West leads the eight of diamonds against your slam. How do you plan the play?

Exercise 2

♠ A 4 3
♡ A Q J 5
◇ 7 6 5 4
♣ 8 3

Match-point pairs

N–S game, dealer South

South	West	North	East
1◇	Pass	1♡	Pass
1NT	Pass	3NT	Pass
Pass	Pass		

♠ K J 8
♡ K 4
◇ A K Q 2
♣ 10 6 5 4

West leads the two of clubs to his partner's ace. East continues with the queen and then the jack of clubs, West following. What do you discard from dummy?

Exercises

Exercise 3

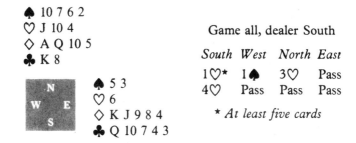

♠ 10 7 6 2
♡ J 10 4
◇ A Q 10 5
♣ K 8

♠ 5 3
♡ 6
◇ K J 9 8 4
♣ Q 10 7 4 3

Game all, dealer South

South	West	North	East
1♡*	1♠	3♡	Pass
4♡	Pass	Pass	Pass

* At least five cards

West starts with the ace, king and three of hearts. You discard a club and a diamond, and South overtakes the third heart with his queen. He then plays the six of diamonds to the seven, ten and jack. What do you return?

Exercise 4

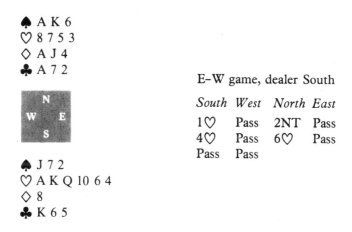

♠ A K 6
♡ 8 7 5 3
◇ A J 4
♣ A 7 2

♠ J 7 2
♡ A K Q 10 6 4
◇ 8
♣ K 6 5

E–W game, dealer South

South	West	North	East
1♡	Pass	2NT	Pass
4♡	Pass	6♡	Pass
Pass	Pass		

West leads the king of diamonds. How do you plan the play?

Exercise 5

♠ 7 6 3
♡ J 7 5
◇ A K J 8 2
♣ A 9

Game all, dealer North

West	North	East	South
	1◇	Pass	4NT *
Pass	5♣**	Pass	7NT
Pass	Pass	Pass	

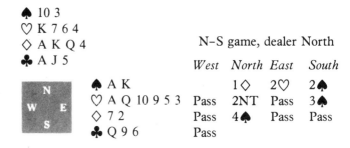

♠ A K Q 5 4
♡ A 8
◇ Q 5
♣ K Q J 7

* *Roman Key-Card Blackwood*
** *0 or 3 key cards*

West leads the king of hearts to your ace. How do you plan the play?

Exercise 6

♠ 10 3
♡ K 7 6 4
◇ A K Q 4
♣ A J 5

N–S game, dealer North

♠ A K
♡ A Q 10 9 5 3
◇ 7 2
♣ Q 9 6

West	North	East	South
	1◇	2♡	2♠
Pass	2NT	Pass	3♠
Pass	4♠	Pass	Pass
Pass			

West leads the eight of hearts, the four is played from dummy and South drops the jack under your queen. How should you continue?

Exercises

Exercise 7

♠ K Q 10 4
♡ Q 8 5
◇ K 7 6 3
♣ A K

♠ A 7 5
♡ A 10
◇ A 9 4
♣ Q J 10 8 5

Game all, dealer South

South	West	North	East
1♣	Pass	1◇	Pass
1NT	Pass	6NT	Pass
Pass	Pass		

West leads the queen of diamonds and you play low from both hands. West continues with the jack of diamonds to your ace. East, having followed the first time, discards the four of clubs. How do you plan the play?

Exercise 8

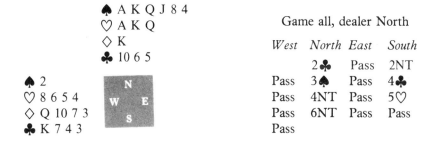

♠ A K Q J 8 4
♡ A K Q
◇ K
♣ 10 6 5

♠ 2
♡ 8 6 5 4
◇ Q 10 7 3
♣ K 7 4 3

Game all, dealer North

West	North	East	South
	2♣	Pass	2NT
Pass	3♠	Pass	4♣
Pass	4NT	Pass	5♡
Pass	6NT	Pass	Pass
Pass			

You try a bold lead of the three of clubs, striking oil when partner's jack forces out declarer's ace. South plays on spades, East following three times while you discard a club and a diamond. On the next spade East throws the two of hearts and South the four of diamonds. Plan your discards.

[99]

Exercise 9

♠ Q 8 4 3
♡ 6 5
◇ 8 7
♣ A K 9 5 4

Game all, dealer East

West	North	East	South
		1♡	Dble
Pass	3♣	Pass	5◇
Pass	Pass	Pass	

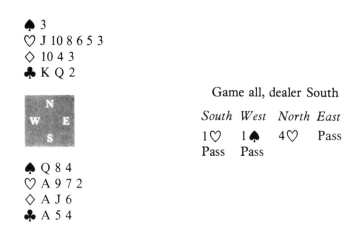

♠ A 10
♡ A 10 3
◇ K Q J 10 9 6 4
♣ 6

West leads the king of hearts and you hold off, hoping for a continuation. No, West switches meanly to a trump. East takes his ace and plays a second trump, West following. How do you plan the play?

Exercise 10

♠ 3
♡ J 10 8 6 5 3
◇ 10 4 3
♣ K Q 2

Game all, dealer South

South	West	North	East
1♡	1♠	4♡	Pass
Pass	Pass		

♠ Q 8 4
♡ A 9 7 2
◇ A J 6
♣ A 5 4

The opening lead is the king of spades on which East plays the jack. West switches to the ten of clubs and you win in dummy with the queen, East contributing the seven. When you play a trump the queen appears from East. You win with the ace and continue with a second trump to West's king, East discarding the two of spades. West perseveres with the nine of clubs. How do you propose to make ten tricks?

Exercise 11

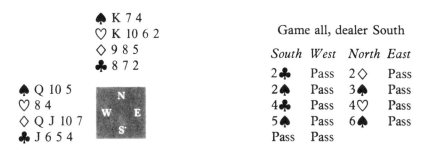

♠ K 7 4
♡ K 10 6 2
◇ 9 8 5
♣ 8 7 2

♠ Q 10 5
♡ 8 4
◇ Q J 10 7
♣ J 6 5 4

Game all, dealer South

South	West	North	East
2♣	Pass	2◇	Pass
2♠	Pass	3♠	Pass
4♣	Pass	4♡	Pass
5♠	Pass	6♠	Pass
Pass	Pass		

You lead the queen of diamonds on which East plays the three and South the ace. East follows suit when a spade is played to the king but discards the three of hearts on the second round. South wins with the ace and continues with a third spade to your queen, East discarding the two of diamonds. How should you continue?

Exercise 12

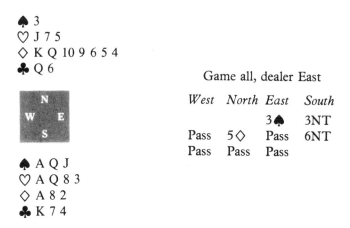

♠ 3
♡ J 7 5
◇ K Q 10 9 6 5 4
♣ Q 6

♠ A Q J
♡ A Q 8 3
◇ A 8 2
♣ K 7 4

Game all, dealer East

West	North	East	South
		3♠	3NT
Pass	5◇	Pass	6NT
Pass	Pass	Pass	

West leads the eight of spades which runs to your jack. How do you plan the play?

Exercise 13

♠ A K 5
♡ A 7
◇ A J 5
♣ A J 9 4 3

Love all, dealer North

West	North	East	South
		2NT	Pass	4♣ *
Pass	4◇**	Pass	7♡
Pass	Pass	Pass	

♠ 10 6 3
♡ K Q 10 9 8 5 3 2
◇ 10
♣ 6

* *Gerber*
** *0 or 4 aces*

West leads the nine of spades to dummy's king. How do you plan the play?

Exercise 14

♠ A 9 2
♡ 10 6 4 2
◇ 8 5
♣ A K J 3

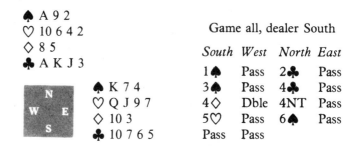

♠ K 7 4
♡ Q J 9 7
◇ 10 3
♣ 10 7 6 5

Game all, dealer South

South	West	North	East
1♠	Pass	2♣	Pass
3♠	Pass	4♣	Pass
4◇	Dble	4NT	Pass
5♡	Pass	6♠	Pass
Pass	Pass		

West leads the eight of hearts and declarer wins with the king. The queen of spades is run and you allow it to hold the trick. On the next spade West shows out and the ace is played. You win the spade king on the third round as West completes an echo in diamonds. What do you return?

Exercise 15

♠ Q J 6
♡ A 5
◇ K 10 9 4
♣ K 7 6 2

Match-point pairs

Game all, dealer South

South	West	North	East
1NT	Pass	3NT	Pass
Pass	Pass		

♠ 7 4 3
♡ K Q J 2
◇ A J 7
♣ A 8 5

West leads the ten of spades, showing two higher cards or none. All doubts are dispelled when East captures dummy's jack with the king. East returns the jack of clubs to dummy's king and you play the diamonds the safe way—low to the ace and then the jack. West covers with the queen of diamonds and you win with the king. How should you continue?

Exercise 16

♠ J 5
♡ A Q 10 9 4
◇ 8 6
♣ A K Q 3

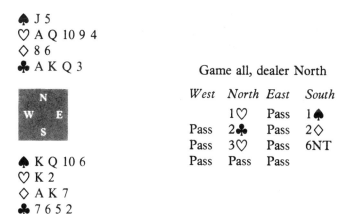

Game all, dealer North

West	North	East	South
	1♡	Pass	1♠
Pass	2♣	Pass	2◇
Pass	3♡	Pass	6NT
Pass	Pass	Pass	

♠ K Q 10 6
♡ K 2
◇ A K 7
♣ 7 6 5 2

West leads the jack of clubs to dummy's queen and East discards the three of spades. You test the hearts with the king and ace, and West throws the four of clubs on the second round. Next you try the jack of spades but nobody wants this trick, East playing the two and West the four. How should you continue?

Exercise 17

♠ 2
♡ A 6 3
◇ A K J 8 4 3
♣ 8 5 2

Love all, dealer North

West	North	East	South
	1 ◇	Pass	2 ♠
Pass	3 ◇	Pass	4NT
Pass	5 ♡	Pass	5NT
Pass	6 ◇	Pass	7 ♠
Pass	Pass	Pass	

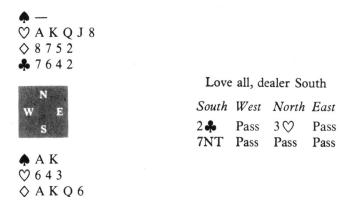

♠ 8 3
♡ 9 7 4
◇ Q 10 6 5
♣ K J 9 4

West leads the queen of hearts to declarer's king. South plays the ace, king and queen of spades, discarding a club and a diamond from the table. West follows three times and you discard a club on the third round. Next comes a diamond to the ace and the king of diamonds, South discarding the club. A third diamond is ruffed, West discarding the two of hearts, and when South continues with the jack of spades West discards the five of hearts. Plan your discards on the long trumps.

Exercise 18

♠ —
♡ A K Q J 8
◇ 8 7 5 2
♣ 7 6 4 2

Love all, dealer South

South	West	North	East
2 ♣	Pass	3 ♡	Pass
7NT	Pass	Pass	Pass

♠ A K
♡ 6 4 3
◇ A K Q 6
♣ A K Q 8

West leads the jack of spades. You discard a diamond from dummy and win with the king. When you play a heart to dummy's jack West discards a spade. How do you plan the play?

Exercise 19

♠ Q 6 2
♡ Q 5
◇ 10 7 6 4
♣ A 7 5 4

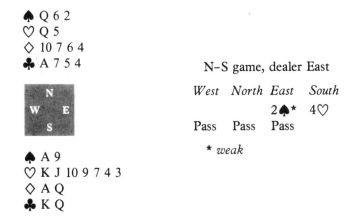

N–S game, dealer East

West	North	East	South
		2♠*	4♡
Pass	Pass	Pass	

* *weak*

♠ A 9
♡ K J 10 9 7 4 3
◇ A Q
♣ K Q

West leads the eight of spades to the two, ten and ace. When you play the jack of hearts at trick two, East wins with the ace and returns the two of hearts, West following both times. How do you plan the play?

Exercise 20

♠ A Q J 9 8 7
♡ K 5 4
◇ 3
♣ A 9 5

♠ K 10 6 5 2
♡ 8 7
◇ 9 7 4
♣ Q 6 3

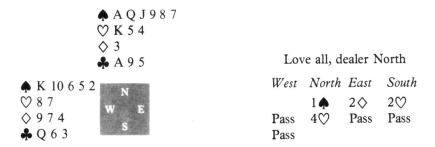

Love all, dealer North

West	North	East	South
	1♠	2◇	2♡
Pass	4♡	Pass	Pass
Pass			

You lead the seven of diamonds and partner wins with the king. East switches to the ace of hearts and continues with the heart two. South wins with the queen and plays the three of spades to dummy's jack. Next comes the seven of spades, on which both East and South discard diamonds. In with the ten of spades, how do you continue?

Solution 1

From the lead it appears that both diamond honours are offside. Perhaps West has done you a favour by making this plain. Naturally you must put in the ten of diamonds and allow East to win the first trick. This will rectify the count for any squeeze that may be needed.

Win the spade return in hand and test the hearts. If the suit breaks evenly you have twelve tricks. In practice East shows out on the third round of hearts, and you have to play for a positional double squeeze with spades as the double menace. The single threat against East must lie in your own hand, so you must hope that West began with no more than two diamonds. Cash the ace of diamonds to unblock the suit before running the clubs. The full hand:

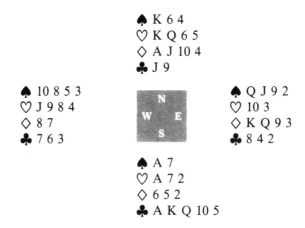

```
              ♠ K 6 4
              ♡ K Q 6 5
              ◇ A J 10 4
              ♣ J 9
♠ 10 8 5 3                    ♠ Q J 9 2
♡ J 9 8 4         N          ♡ 10 3
◇ 8 7          W     E        ◇ K Q 9 3
♣ 7 6 3           S          ♣ 8 4 2
              ♠ A 7
              ♡ A 7 2
              ◇ 6 5 2
              ♣ A K Q 10 5
```

When you play the last club, West has to keep the heart jack and East the diamond king. Neither can retain two spades, and the six of spades becomes your twelfth trick.

Solution 2

The contract is in no danger, and an overtrick could come from an even diamond split, a successful spade finesse or a squeeze. To keep your options open you should discard a diamond from dummy on the third club.

Win East's diamond switch and cash a second top diamond. It comes as no big surprise when West discards a heart on the second round. What should you do now?

The simple answer is to lay down your hand and claim ten tricks. There is no need to rely on the spade finesse, for you can squeeze out that tenth trick for sure. You have a club menace against West, a diamond menace against East, and a split three-card double menace in spades. Just cash the third top diamond and then play hearts, discarding the spade eight on the third round. Neither defender will be able to cope when the fourth heart is led, and dummy's four of spades will take the tenth trick. The complete deal:

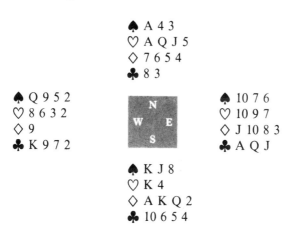

```
              ♠ A 4 3
              ♡ A Q J 5
              ◇ 7 6 5 4
              ♣ 8 3
♠ Q 9 5 2              ♠ 10 7 6
♡ 8 6 3 2     N        ♡ 10 9 7
◇ 9        W     E     ◇ J 10 8 3
♣ K 9 7 2     S        ♣ A Q J
              ♠ K J 8
              ♡ K 4
              ◇ A K Q 2
              ♣ 10 6 5 4
```

Note there would have been no squeeze if you had carelessly discarded a spade from dummy on the third club.

Solution 3

It seems natural to switch to spades in the hope of promoting a trick in partner's suit. However, since you have the diamond situation under control declarer's spade loser can hardly run away. Moreover, it is highly likely that South will have the ace and king of spades and the ace of clubs for his bidding. Four hearts, two spades, two clubs and a diamond will give him nine tricks, and the tenth may come from a positional double squeeze using a split three-card menace in clubs.

An attack on the double menace is the right medicine. If you can take out the king of clubs, declarer will have nothing left but an inverted positional squeeze which will fail because dummy has no entry in spades.

A further point. You have to hope that partner has the jack of clubs, but if you make him play it at trick five you could still be exposed to a simple squeeze in the minor suits. To avoid this hazard you should switch to the ten or the queen of clubs.

The complete hand:

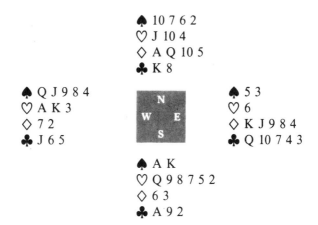

```
                    ♠ 10 7 6 2
                    ♡ J 10 4
                    ◇ A Q 10 5
                    ♣ K 8
♠ Q J 9 8 4                              ♠ 5 3
♡ A K 3              N                    ♡ 6
◇ 7 2            W       E                ◇ K J 9 8 4
♣ J 6 5             S                    ♣ Q 10 7 4 3
                    ♠ A K
                    ♡ Q 9 8 7 5 2
                    ◇ 6 3
                    ♣ A 9 2
```

Solution 4

Eleven tricks are on view and, unless the queen of spades drops in two rounds, the twelfth trick will have to come from a squeeze. A trick has to be conceded to rectify the count, and the time to do it is right now. Play low from dummy at trick one, allowing the king of diamonds to win.

There appears to be a choice of squeezes on this hand. You could try for a simple spade-diamond squeeze against West, but there is no good reason why West should have most of the missing honour cards. It seems better to place the queen of spades with East and opt for the double positional squeeze with clubs as the long menace. A Vienna Coup will be needed to unblock the spades, and you will still succeed if West has the doubleton queen.

Win the club switch in hand with the king, draw trumps, play off the top spades and the ace of diamonds, discarding a club from your hand. Now, if the cards lie as you hope, the run of the trumps will squeeze both opponents.

The full hand:

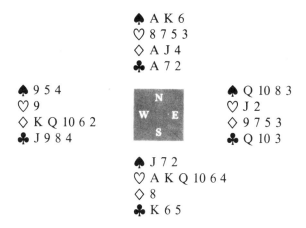

```
                    ♠ A K 6
                    ♡ 8 7 5 3
                    ◇ A J 4
                    ♣ A 7 2
  ♠ 9 5 4                              ♠ Q 10 8 3
  ♡ 9               N                  ♡ J 2
  ◇ K Q 10 6 2    W   E                ◇ 9 7 5 3
  ♣ J 9 8 4         S                  ♣ Q 10 3
                    ♠ J 7 2
                    ♡ A K Q 10 6 4
                    ◇ 8
                    ♣ K 6 5
```

This looks almost too easy. On normal breaks you will have fifteen tricks to juggle with. But it is always wise to assume that the breaks will be bad.

If a squeeze is needed the squeeze card may be the fourth club, so you must retain a card of entry in the opposite hand. It would be a mistake, in other words, to test the diamonds at an early stage. First you should play off two rounds of spades. If East shows out on the second spade, you have a simple major-suit squeeze against West. Run the clubs, discarding a heart and a diamond from dummy, and continue with four rounds of diamonds.

In practice it is West who shows out on the second spade, discarding a club. You have a heart menace against West and a spade menace against East. Hence neither defender will be able to retain a diamond guard should he happen to hold it. Just cash the third spade winner and follow with four rounds of clubs.

Technically this is not a double squeeze, since both opponents cannot hold diamonds. But the form is exactly the same, and you don't really mind which defender you squeeze.

The complete deal:

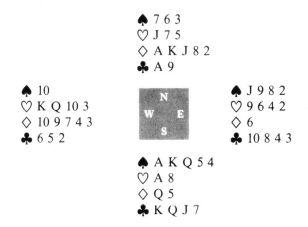

♠ 7 6 3
♥ J 7 5
♦ A K J 8 2
♣ A 9

♠ 10
♥ K Q 10 3
♦ 10 9 7 4 3
♣ 6 5 2

♠ J 9 8 2
♥ 9 6 4 2
♦ 6
♣ 10 8 4 3

♠ A K Q 5 4
♥ A 8
♦ Q 5
♣ K Q J 7

Solution 6

On the bidding it must be highly unlikely that declarer has a second heart, so you must hope to take the setting trick in clubs. To avoid the risk of being end-played, you may think of cashing the top spades and then getting off lead with a diamond. But there is danger in this course. If South has six spades and the king of clubs, as seems likely, he may be able to make ten tricks with the help of a double squeeze.

This time you are unable to attack the double menace because of dummy's tenace in clubs. Fortunately you have an alternative line of defence. If declarer has six trumps partner will have three, and you can make use of these to destroy dummy's heart menace. Continue with the ace of hearts for South to ruff, and lead hearts twice more when you are in with the top spades. South will have to ruff both times and the heart threat will disappear. Partner can then look after the diamonds while you take care of the clubs, and there will be no squeeze.

The full hand:

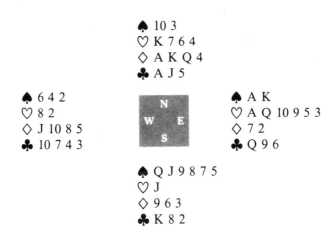

```
              ♠ 10 3
              ♡ K 7 6 4
              ◊ A K Q 4
              ♣ A J 5
♠ 6 4 2              N        ♠ A K
♡ 8 2                        ♡ A Q 10 9 5 3
◊ J 10 8 5     W       E      ◊ 7 2
♣ 10 7 4 3           S        ♣ Q 9 6
              ♠ Q J 9 8 7 5
              ♡ J
              ◊ 9 6 3
              ♣ K 8 2
```

When East shows out on the second diamond your slam is assured. It is just a matter of cashing your tricks in the right order. If the spades break evenly or the jack comes down you will have no problems. If West has long spades, a simple squeeze in spades and diamonds will bring about the happy ending. And if East has the spades you will have an inverted positional double squeeze with hearts as the double menace. You know this squeeze will succeed because you have an entry to dummy in West's suit—diamonds.

The club blockage means you have to be careful with your entries to hand, for you cannot afford to use the ace of hearts. First unblock the clubs, and continue with the king, queen and ace of spades followed by the rest of the clubs. The full hand:

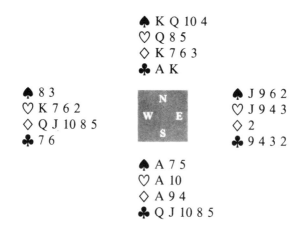

<pre>
                ♠ K Q 10 4
                ♡ Q 8 5
                ◇ K 7 6 3
                ♣ A K
  ♠ 8 3   ♠ J 9 6 2
  ♡ K 7 6 2   N   ♡ J 9 4 3
  ◇ Q J 10 8 5   W   E   ◇ 2
  ♣ 7 6   S   ♣ 9 4 3 2
                ♠ A 7 5
                ♡ A 10
                ◇ A 9 4
                ♣ Q J 10 8 5
</pre>

On the last club West has to bare the king of hearts in order to keep his diamond guard. You throw the small diamond from dummy and play to the king of diamonds to apply pressure to East.

Solution 8

Declarer would have had twelve tricks but for your club lead which took out his entry before he could unblock the diamond king. How can you take advantage of that fortunate lead?

Partner is marked with the queen of clubs and declarer with the nine. The danger is that South may still bring home his slam with the help of a double winkle. The ending will be a three-card one. If you and your partner both keep two clubs and come down to a singleton diamond, declarer will simply overtake the king of diamonds at trick eleven. If you both keep two diamonds and keep one club, he will play the six of clubs from dummy, establishing a trick for dummy's ten. And if one of you keeps two diamonds, the stepping-stone ending will apply. Declarer will unblock the king of diamonds and exit with the low club.

There is no hope if declarer has the jack of diamonds, but if partner has that card you can defeat the slam by throwing two more diamonds and the small club on the spades, keeping your precious fourth heart.

The complete deal:

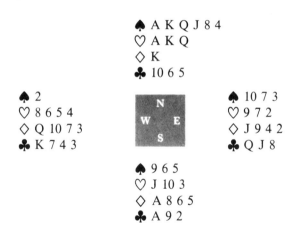

        ♠ A K Q J 8 4
        ♡ A K Q
        ◇ K
        ♣ 10 6 5

♠ 2   ♠ 10 7 3
♡ 8 6 5 4   ♡ 9 7 2
◇ Q 10 7 3   ◇ J 9 4 2
♣ K 7 4 3   ♣ Q J 8

        ♠ 9 6 5
        ♡ J 10 3
        ◇ A 8 6 5
        ♣ A 9 2

They have stopped you from ruffing a heart in dummy but you are not without chances. You have a heart menace against East, and if you had a spade menace against West you would have an automatic double squeeze with clubs as the long menace. On the bidding East is sure to have the king of spades. West could have the jack, however, and you might think of winning the second trump in dummy and playing the queen of spades to force a cover from East. Your menace would then be nicely placed for the double squeeze.

It is good to consider all possibilities, but a double squeeze is not invariably the right answer. There is no merit in complicating simple situations. Here you have a straightforward major-suit squeeze against East irrespective of the location of the jack of spades. Just run the diamonds, discarding three clubs and two spades from the table. Cash one of the major-suit aces to avoid ambiguity, then play the top clubs to apply the pressure. The full hand:

```
                  ♠ Q 8 4 3
                  ♡ 6 5
                  ◇ 8 7
                  ♣ A K 9 5 4
  ♠ 9 7 6 5 2            N          ♠ K J
  ♡ K 7            W          E     ♡ Q J 9 8 4 2
  ◇ 5 3                 S          ◇ A 2
  ♣ J 8 7 3                         ♣ Q 10 2
                  ♠ A 10
                  ♡ A 10 3
                  ◇ K Q J 10 9 6 4
                  ♣ 6
```

Solution 10

A second diamond trick is all you need. Routine play will succeed if East has both honours, while if West has them both you can organise an end-play after eliminating the clubs. But it is more likely that the diamond honours will be split, and you cannot hope for a 5–2 division in the suit. All the indications are that East began with a 4–1–4–4 shape.

What is left? Well, East has kindly told you that he has the ten of spades. If he has the nine as well, you should be able to squeeze both defenders in diamonds and spades.

At present you have two losers and you cannot afford to rectify the count. If you duck a diamond the suit will be returned, removing a vital entry from your hand. Fortunately the double ruffing squeeze will work perfectly well with two losers. Win the second club in dummy and play three more rounds of trumps, discarding a diamond from hand. The play of a club to your ace will apply the pressure. The complete deal:

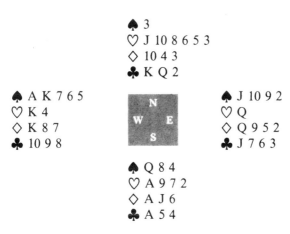

```
                    ♠ 3
                    ♡ J 10 8 6 5 3
                    ◇ 10 4 3
                    ♣ K Q 2
  ♠ A K 7 6 5                        ♠ J 10 9 2
  ♡ K 4              N               ♡ Q
  ◇ K 8 7        W       E           ◇ Q 9 5 2
  ♣ 10 9 8           S               ♣ J 7 6 3
                    ♠ Q 8 4
                    ♡ A 9 7 2
                    ◇ A J 6
                    ♣ A 5 4
```

If either defender reduces to a singleton spade, you establish a spade trick with a ruff. If both keep two spades, you continue with the ace and jack of diamonds. Note that the squeeze will work even if one defender has both diamond honours.

The distribution is pretty well marked. South has a 6–2–2–3 shape and he will not be missing an ace or a king. That gives him eleven top tricks, and if you continue hopefully with a second diamond he is bound to make his twelfth trick with the help of a double squeeze. It is the inverted automatic type of squeeze which will practically play itself. Declarer will discard two clubs and a heart on the trumps and the defence will be helpless.

The only chance is to attack the double menace by switching to a low club. This removes an idle card from dummy and converts the squeeze into a positional one which will fail because the entry to dummy is in the wrong red suit.

The full hand:

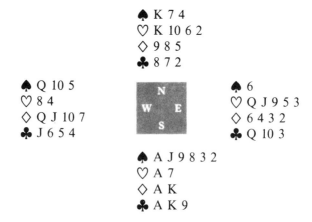

The club switch may look dangerous but this is not really the case. If declarer's clubs are as good as A K 10 he is going to make his slam anyway.

Solution 12

You have ten top tricks and can develop an eleventh in clubs. The twelfth might come from hearts. If you play a club at trick two and the queen wins, for instance, you might develop an end-play against West.

But East is likely to have one of the missing honours—the club ace or the heart king—for his vulnerable three-bid. If East wins the ace of clubs at trick two and returns a heart, you can go up with the ace, cash the ace of spades and run the diamonds to enforce a double squeeze. Unfortunately a real bridge player in the East seat will return not a heart but a club and your double squeeze will evaporate.

Slipping past the ace of clubs is a good idea, but you have to do it the other way round. Play a diamond to dummy at trick two and return the six of clubs. If West captures your king with the ace, you can bank on East being squeezed in the majors. If the club king wins, run six more diamonds and continue with a heart to your ace. If he has kept two spades East must have bared the ace of clubs and the throw-in yields the twelfth trick.

The complete hand:

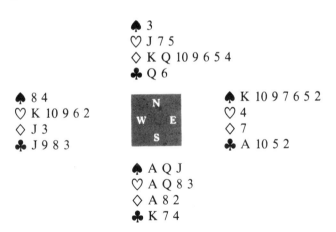

```
              ♠ 3
              ♡ J 7 5
              ◇ K Q 10 9 6 5 4
              ♣ Q 6
♠ 8 4                          ♠ K 10 9 7 6 5 2
♡ K 10 9 6 2      N            ♡ 4
◇ J 3         W       E        ◇ 7
♣ J 9 8 3         S            ♣ A 10 5 2
              ♠ A Q J
              ♡ A Q 8 3
              ◇ A 8 2
              ♣ K 7 4
```

The double squeeze should not be regarded as a cure for all ills.

Solution 13

You are in a fine contract. There are twelve top tricks and you will naturally expect to develop the thirteenth trick in clubs. Even if the clubs break badly, squeeze play will make a certainty of the grand slam since East is marked with the missing spade honours.

The sequence of play should be: a heart to the king, club to the ace, club ruff (with the queen if you can afford it), heart to the ace, club ruff. If West shows out you have a simple ruffing squeeze against East. Play off all the trumps but one, discarding two diamonds and a spade from dummy. A diamond to the ace will then make East's task impossible.

In practice it is East who shows out on the third club since the full hand is as follows:

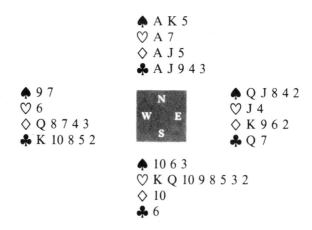

```
              ♠ A K 5
              ♡ A 7
              ◇ A J 5
              ♣ A J 9 4 3

  ♠ 9 7                        ♠ Q J 8 4 2
  ♡ 6          N              ♡ J 4
  ◇ Q 8 7 4 3  W   E          ◇ K 9 6 2
  ♣ K 10 8 5 2    S           ♣ Q 7

              ♠ 10 6 3
              ♡ K Q 10 9 8 5 3 2
              ◇ 10
              ♣ 6
```

After ruffing the third club, you cross to the king of spades, ruff another club and play out the rest of the trumps to inflict the double squeeze.

Solution 14

It seems natural to return a diamond in response to partner's double, but what is natural is not always right. South can be counted for five spade tricks, two hearts, one diamond and three clubs with the help of the finesse. What about his shape? West's echo in diamonds shows an even number, obviously six, and you know him to have started with two hearts and one spade. That gives him four clubs, leaving declarer with a singleton.

The danger is becoming clear. If you return a diamond (or a heart) declarer will simply rattle off the rest of his winners to achieve a double squeeze. West will have to keep a winning diamond, you will have to keep the heart queen, and neither of you will be able to retain four clubs in the ending.

To defeat this slam you must attack the double menace, making the unnatural-looking return of a club into dummy's tenace holding. With his communications in disarray, declarer will then have no play for the slam.

The complete deal:

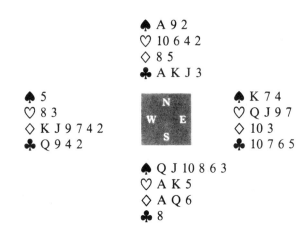

```
              ♠ A 9 2
              ♡ 10 6 4 2
              ◇ 8 5
              ♣ A K J 3
  ♠ 5                          ♠ K 7 4
  ♡ 8 3              N         ♡ Q J 9 7
  ◇ K J 9 7 4 2   W     E      ◇ 10 3
  ♣ Q 9 4 2          S         ♣ 10 7 6 5
              ♠ Q J 10 8 6 3
              ♡ A K 5
              ◇ A Q 6
              ♣ 8
```

You are safe for ten tricks but there is no law against trying for a second overtrick. It is just a matter of playing off your winners in the optimum order. First you should run the hearts, discarding two clubs from dummy, and then finish the diamonds. Both defenders are squeezed in the black suits when the complete deal turns out to be:

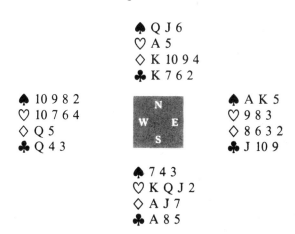

```
                    ♠ Q J 6
                    ♡ A 5
                    ◇ K 10 9 4
                    ♣ K 7 6 2
   ♠ 10 9 8 2                        ♠ A K 5
   ♡ 10 7 6 4          N             ♡ 9 8 3
   ◇ Q 5           W       E         ◇ 8 6 3 2
   ♣ Q 4 3             S             ♣ J 10 9
                    ♠ 7 4 3
                    ♡ K Q J 2
                    ◇ A J 7
                    ♣ A 8 5
```

If East discards his small spade on the last diamond, you throw the eight of clubs from hand and play the low spade from the table. If East discards a club instead, you throw a spade from hand and watch West squirm as the jaws of the vice close around him. When he eventually lets go one of his spade equals, you return to the ace of clubs and play your spade to the ten, queen and ace. The last trick belongs to the six of spades in dummy.

Solution 16

When the ace of spades has gone you will have eleven tricks and can hope to make a twelfth by means of an inverted automatic double squeeze. But the squeeze will remain intact only as long as you have two top diamonds in hand. It seems highly likely that whoever wins the ace of spades will switch to a diamond, converting the squeeze to a positional one which will fail if the queen of hearts has not been played off.

East in particular is sure to switch to a diamond (he can hardly return a heart), which means you are not likely to make the slam when East has the spade ace.

That being the case, you may as well ensure success when West has the spade ace. Cash the queen of hearts, discarding a club from hand, before playing a second spade.

The full hand:

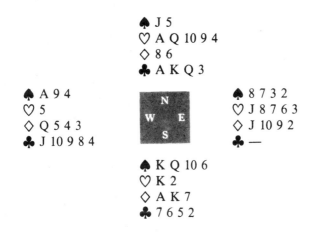

```
                    ♠ J 5
                    ♡ A Q 10 9 4
                    ◇ 8 6
                    ♣ A K Q 3
   ♠ A 9 4                          ♠ 8 7 3 2
   ♡ 5             N                ♡ J 8 7 6 3
   ◇ Q 5 4 3    W     E             ◇ J 10 9 2
   ♣ J 10 9 8 4    S                ♣ —
                    ♠ K Q 10 6
                    ♡ K 2
                    ◇ A K 7
                    ♣ 7 6 5 2
```

Now a diamond return cannot hurt. You simply play the remaining spades, squeezing first West and then East in the inverted positional ending.

Solution 17

South can be counted for seven spade tricks, two hearts, two diamonds and the ace of clubs. If he has the queen of clubs along with his ace he is bound to make thirteen tricks. If his second club is a lower card he is booked for defeat, since there is no genuine squeeze on the hand.

But you still have to exercise proper care. If you try to hang on to your clubs, you will transform the pseudo-squeeze into a live inverted positional double squeeze. Partner, left to guard the hearts, will have to bare his queen of clubs on the play of the last spade. The small heart will be thrown from the table and the ace of hearts will squeeze you in the minors.

Clearly you must keep your hearts and discard clubs, and it will help to clarify matters for partner if you throw the king of clubs on the fourth spade. The complete hand:

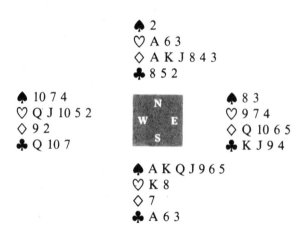

```
                    ♠ 2
                    ♡ A 6 3
                    ◇ A K J 8 4 3
                    ♣ 8 5 2
♠ 10 7 4                              ♠ 8 3
♡ Q J 10 5 2            N             ♡ 9 7 4
◇ 9 2             W          E        ◇ Q 10 6 5
♣ Q 10 7               S             ♣ K J 9 4
                    ♠ A K Q J 9 6 5
                    ♡ K 8
                    ◇ 7
                    ♣ A 6 3
```

A good rule to follow in pseudo-squeeze situations is to keep the suits that are held on your right, discarding those held on your left.

Solution 18

It is no more than a minor nuisance when the hearts prove to be 5–0. The grand slam is still on ice even if both minor suits also break badly.

The simplest way to continue is by testing the clubs next. If East proves to have club length, you have an automatic squeeze against him in clubs and hearts. Cash the top diamonds and the ace of spades, discarding a club from dummy.

If West proves to hold the clubs, the defenders are ripe for an 'Either-Or' squeeze. Cash the third club winner, play the ace of spades, discarding another diamond from the table, and run the hearts, discarding the club from hand. You care not at all who, if anyone, has length in diamonds. Either East will be squeezed in the red suits or West will be squeezed in the minors.

The complete deal:

```
                    ♠ —
                    ♡ A K Q J 8
                    ◇ 8 7 5 2
                    ♣ 7 6 4 2
    ♠ J 10 9 5 4              ♠ Q 8 7 6 3 2
    ♡ —           N           ♡ 10 9 7 5 2
    ◇ J 10 4 3  W   E         ◇ 9
    ♣ J 9 5 3      S          ♣ 10
                    ♠ A K
                    ♡ 6 4 3
                    ♡ A K Q 6
                    ♣ A K Q 8
```

Solution 19

East has defended well by refusing to let you unblock the clubs, and it's no good hoping for the diamond finesse to succeed. East has already shown up with enough points for his weak two bid, and West is marked with the king of diamonds.

However, if you can read the ending accurately, you should be able to make ten tricks with the help of a double stepping-stone. You have a spade menace against East, a diamond menace against West and a double threat in clubs. Just cash the ace of diamonds and trundle out the trumps to put the defenders under pressure.

The full hand:

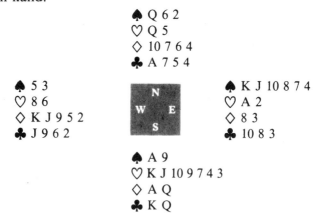

```
                ♠ Q 6 2
                ♡ Q 5
                ◇ 10 7 6 4
                ♣ A 7 5 4
  ♠ 5 3                      ♠ K J 10 8 7 4
  ♡ 8 6          N           ♡ A 2
  ◇ K J 9 5 2  W   E         ◇ 8 3
  ♣ J 9 6 2       S          ♣ 10 8 3
                ♠ A 9
                ♡ K J 10 9 7 4 3
                ◇ A Q
                ♣ K Q
```

On the play of the last trump neither defender will be able to keep three clubs, his own winner *and* a card in his partner's suit. In the most likely ending you will unblock the clubs and then exit towards the defender who has a club left.

Solution 20

On the line of play adopted, declarer appears to have a 1–5–4–3 shape, and it is clear that a trump lead would have given the defence a better start. Can you recover?

South is sure to have the king of clubs, and he has nine tricks if you count a diamond ruff in dummy. The danger is that the tenth trick may come from a double squeeze. If you return a diamond, for instance, declarer will ruff on the table, ruff a spade and play two more rounds of trumps, forcing you to part with a club. A club to the ace will be followed by the ace of spades, squeezing partner in the minors.

What is needed is an attack on the double menace in clubs, but a club lead risks giving declarer three tricks in the suit when his clubs are as good as K 10 x. You can afford to concede three club tricks only if you make it impossible for South to enjoy the ace of spades. You should therefore switch to the club queen. The full hand:

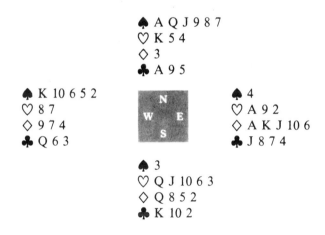

```
              ♠ A Q J 9 8 7
              ♡ K 5 4
              ◇ 3
              ♣ A 9 5

♠ K 10 6 5 2        N        ♠ 4
♡ 8 7          W       E      ♡ A 9 2
◇ 9 7 4             S        ◇ A K J 10 6
♣ Q 6 3                      ♣ J 8 7 4

              ♠ 3
              ♡ Q J 10 6 3
              ◇ Q 8 5 2
              ♣ K 10 2
```

In order to score three club tricks declarer has to win on the table with the ace, but East's remaining trump keeps the ace of spades at bay and puts the contract one down.

Fortunately defence is not always so difficult!